BELIEF TO

PURSUIT

ELIZABETH NAPIER

SAVED IN CHRIST PUBLICATIONS

Belief to Pursuit

Published in Carleton, MI by Saved in Christ Publications. For fundraising opportunities, wholesale purchase, or educational use please email savedsisterinchrist@gmail.com.

Unless otherwise indicated, all biblical quotations in this book are from the World English Bible, American English Edition, without Strong's numbers.

ISBN: 979-8-9881040-2-5
Library of Congress Control Number: 2023914328

Cover and interior design: Elizabeth Napier. Cover Image by Foundry Co. from Pixabay.

1 2 3 4 5 6 7 8 9 10

All honor and praise belong to Almighty God, and I thank Him for allowing me to write this book to glorify His name. I am grateful for His Holy Spirit that guides me as I pursue His Heavenly kingdom, and for the family and friends He has brought into my life, who have made this journey all the more pleasant and filled with love.

TABLE OF CONTENTS

1
INTRODUCTION

"You shall call on me, and you shall go and pray to me, and I will listen to you. You shall seek me and find me, when you search for me with all your heart."
- Jeremiah 29:12-13

"My son, if you will receive my words, and store up my commandments within you, so as to turn your ear to wisdom, and apply your heart to understanding; yes, if you call out for discernment, and lift up your voice for understanding; if you seek her as silver, and search for her as for hidden treasures; then you will understand the fear of Yahweh, and find the knowledge of God."
- Proverbs 2:1-5

In the first book in this series, *Logic to Belief,* we explored the idea of why it makes sense to believe in God, and the importance of learning about God's word. In this book, we will begin the journey of growing and evolving our faith. The goal is to develop our understanding of what it means to pursue a relationship with God, and how to do it. We will look at what we learn in the Bible about how we have been saved from death, and think about the choices we must make in order to be confident we will reach an eternal life with God.

At the end of *Logic to Belief,* readers were invited to pray a version of a sinner's prayer. This generally involves admitting to, and repenting of your sins and asking the Lord for forgiveness. It includes forgiving others for their sins against you, and thanking God for what He has done already in your life. Most significantly, it declares your hope by proclaiming your belief in salvation through Jesus Christ, and asking for His Holy Spirit to come into your heart and change you. Throughout this book, we will come to a much deeper knowledge of what is happening within and around us when we pray these words with a sincere heart, and why each of the actions of the prayer are vital.

When I first began my faith journey, I honestly had very little idea of what to expect. I knew a bit about "religion" but I soon realized I knew far less than I thought I did about God. Things started happening that I did not anticipate, and that dramatically changed my life. As I read the Bible for the first time, I quickly noticed how much of it was misused and/or misunderstood by people. Most of the time, when I saw people on social media attacking Christianity, I would realize they had based their attacks on false or misquoted information. I also realized that I had been guilty of doing the same, before I read and understood it for myself. My initial perceptions were being shattered as I read and learned the truth, and my own misconceptions were corrected.

My expectations of what following God would entail, turned out to be much different from how I eventually learned things work. I suppose I expected an instantaneous change in my behavior and attitude the moment I accepted God. That suddenly, all of my anger, doubt, fear, and pain would disappear, and I would be miraculously perfect. This sort of happened, but also did not happen. In that moment when God entered my life, I found I was somehow substantially different, but also almost exactly the same. Part of me changed instantly. I was overcome with a desire to know everything I could about God and to do what was right in His sight, but that was easier said than done. I knew certain things I did were wrong, but I still needed to go through the refinement process, so I could learn how to let go of my sinful desires and behaviors. This is a difficult concept to explain, but I think you will come to understand what I mean as you read this book and begin to go through this journey yourself. Because, as you will find out, it is quite a journey when you start to actively pursue God's kingdom. We have to walk a long path with the Lord, and there are many twists and turns and unexpected surprises along the way.

I assume that if you are reading this book, you probably already believe or are very open to believing in God and eternal life with Him. Perhaps you think you believe, but you still have some questions about what that means, or about what you should do next. The ultimate goal of this book is to guide you as you take your first cautious steps on your faith journey. Whenever I reached some new milestone on my walk with Christ, I sought out resources and searched for explanations for all of the "crazy" things that I was experiencing (like why did I have these embarrassing, uncontrollable tears streaming down my face every time I worshiped?). I eventually found out my crazy experiences were shared by other believers, but I still felt quite discombobulated for a while. I was learning a whole new vocabulary, and struggling to put all of the pieces together. I had to learn to open my mind to seeing things in a different light - God's light. It was like everything I had once known now seemed strange, and I felt out of place in the world, but still also drawn to aspects of it. While apparently that feeling is common, it didn't always seem like anyone else was aware of the overwhelming things that were happening to me. I had trouble fathoming that it was all real. I knew what God was telling me, but I didn't realize fully that this was how it is supposed to work. I would have appreciated a guide with everything in one place, explaining the process to me, without any particular "religious" agenda. In this book, I will attempt to help you think through each facet of getting started on your journey with God, along with sharing some details from my own experiences, in the hopes that you find it a useful tool.

One thing I should point out is that when writing this type of book, it is easy for authors to come off as preachy sounding, or sanctimonious. Please know in my heart that is not my intention. I want to make it very clear that there is nothing about me that makes me better or worse than anyone else in this world. I was a horrible sinner who became a child of God. The only reason I am saved is through God's grace, mercy, and love, and the sacrifice of Jesus Christ, the same as everyone else. I do not deserve or desire any praise, because anything I have been able to accomplish has solely been due to the help and blessing of Almighty God. I was guilty too and needed His salvation. Anything I say in this, or any other book, applies as equally to me as it does to all of you, and is usually born out of my own experiences. For example whenever I mention road rage, I'm working on myself! I write because I am doing my best to obey God's directive, not because I am a perfect person. I am trying to share my experiences and apply them universally, to help other people find what I have found.

You may have noticed that I put the words "religion" or "religious" in quotes above. Let's quickly define these here so I can stop doing that. When I use the term religion or its derivations, I mean it in the sense of all of the various rules and traditions that are wrapped up in each denomination: the lighting of candles in a certain way, the garments and hierarchies, the mindless rituals, and memorized worship. These are all things that can be used to exclude people who aren't familiar with them. They also risk desensitizing those who know them too well, and thus end up only going through the motions. I knew when to stand, when to kneel, and had all of the prayers memorized when I was a youth in church, but I didn't know God. God exists outside of any sort of religious framework. Many so-called religious practices and traditions, currently in use by some churches, are never mentioned in the Bible, and some actually go against what is written. Throughout the Bible, Jesus consistently chastises the religious leaders for using all of their rituals, rules, and laws to judge and condemn one another. He calls out their hypocrisy, and reminds us that performing all of the most religious practices we can think of, is not the way we receive salvation. We were not saved by attending church every Sunday and Wednesday, or by any of our own actions. We were saved by the Lord, and we must develop our own relationship with Him. Through that relationship, we will be cleansed and transformed. Therefore, this book does not endorse any particular religion or religious practice, only following the truth of the Bible. As discussed in *Logic to Belief*, our focus should be on God's word rather than any particular religious agenda.

It is also extremely important to note that this journey involves a long, winding road, with wrong turns, roadblocks, u-turns, and roundabouts. The chapters and activities in these books are not meant to be neat little step-by-step guides to being a Christian. There is no formula for how to approach your journey with God; it involves spending time with Him and getting to know Him as you walk the path together. I struggled with when and where to discuss certain topics, and ultimately asked God.

His clear answer was to write in the order of my own personal experiences. There is not any particular timetable that things will happen in this process, but I have tried my best to break down what happened to me as I walked the path from half-heartedly believing in God, to fully giving my life over to Him. Other people may have followed this path in a slightly different way, or in a different time-frame, but we all share the experience of finally hearing His voice call out to us, and running down the path to meet Him. So please, rather than a rigid checklist, think of these topics as principles, tools, and support, recognizing that you will go back and forth on your journey. One day you will feel like you made so much progress, and then the next day you will feel lost in the woods, unsure of which direction to go. Trust that both of these situations are perfectly normal places to find yourself as you walk with God. You can also trust that no matter where you find yourself, God will be there with you.

Of course, please do not merely rely on me, my critics, or on any one person or group as the sole source of your guidance. Pray for God to reveal Himself to you, to help you understand His plan. Pray for guidance and growth from the Holy Spirit, read the Bible, and listen to what God says to you. There are so many small details that God changes in our lives, that it would be impossible for any person to properly cover everything in a few books. You will need to go to God often, because the answers to your questions cannot always be found in books or sermons written by others. Remember as you read and struggle with these concepts, that God loves you. Remember that anytime you need guidance or support, you can pray to God and ask Him for help.

Before we dive in, please allow me to tell you a short story:

There once was a man who had a beautiful daughter. He loved his little girl so much, he thought his heart would burst. He took care of his daughter, playing, teaching, and nurturing her as she grew. He was kind, gentle, and patient, but also firm when he needed to be, and he made sure his daughter would know life's important rules. As parents do, he taught his daughter manners, to stay away from drugs, not to talk to strangers, and he helped her with her schoolwork as she grew older. The father took care of all of the household bills. He made sure his daughter always had plenty to eat, and nice, suitable, clean clothes to wear. He played soccer with her in the backyard, and made everyone laugh at family game night. He sat with her all night when she was sick, and rushed her to the hospital when emergencies arose. He taught his daughter to do chores, and the value of an honest day's work. As his daughter grew into a teenager, he always made sure she had some of the "coolest" things. His daughter and her friends always hung out at his house and loved to get his advice. By all accounts, he was the best father anyone could ever ask for.

But then one day, his daughter started hanging out with a guy she met through some friends. This other man was younger, and cooler than her father. He drove a fast car, and had fun video games and junk food at his apartment. Over time, this man started convincing the daughter that her father was being unreasonable, because he wouldn't let her take the car to stay out all night with her friends, or because he made her do homework, or chores. He allowed the girl and her friends to hang out at his house, doing whatever they wanted. He told them they didn't have to conform to the boring life of work and drudgery that their parents were pressuring them into. They could have way more fun, and a better life if they listened to him. He let them try alcohol, and skip school, and pretty much do all of the things that their parents would not let them do at home. Slowly, but surely, the daughter began to resent her father, and to rebel against the rules in his household. She made up reasons to be away from home, and to spend more and more time at this other man's house. Her grades started slipping, and her father became concerned. He tried to help her, but she yelled at him, and told her father to stop smothering her.

As time went on, the daughter grew increasingly distant from her father, and started drinking more and trying some of the drugs the other kids were doing, getting them from this man. She was fighting with her father all the time, until one day she just left. She told her father that she no longer wanted anything to do with him, that she loved this other man, and that she was moving out. She blocked her father in every way possible and told him to stay out of her life. Her father eventually tracked her down, where she was crashing at the other man's house, and pounded on the door begging her to come home. He even tried calling the police, who brought his daughter home, but that just led to further resentment and to her running away again. Nothing worked. Things continued to get worse for the daughter as she fell deeper and deeper into this lifestyle. She was occasionally arrested for various misdemeanors, and released, and she could often be found sleeping in questionable places.

The father loved his daughter so much he tried anything he could think of to bring her home. He remembered all of the nights he stayed awake with his daughter, taking care of her, and all of the love they shared. He couldn't fathom how quickly it was all taken away, simply because his daughter had listened to the lies of this other man. Why would his daughter choose to give up her life of having everything she ever needed, in exchange for crashing on a couch (or worse), doing whatever she could to get money for food and drugs? Yes she had some rules to follow at home, but they were put in place for her own protection, and they really were not that much of a burden to follow. His daughter had such a bright future ahead, filled with blessings, and a loving father who would go to the ends of the earth for her, but she threw it away for the false promises of the other man.

The father in the story above would do whatever he could to help his daughter. He wants to heal her and accept her back into his household, but he cannot do it if the daughter isn't willing. His daughter would have to make changes so that she could live peacefully with her father and the other members of the household. She would have to leave the other life behind, go to rehab/stop doing drugs, and recommit to her family. The daughter cannot live at her father's house and follow her father's rules, while at the same time living at this other man's house, partying and taking drugs. She has to choose one way of life or the other. The father cannot just allow the daughter to come home without cleaning up first, because she threatens their family members, steals from them to buy drugs, and trashes the house.

The daughter may want to come home sometimes, but she thinks her father will be too angry or disappointed with her to allow her to return. She feels ashamed of the things she has done and fears that she will never be forgiven. On the other hand, there are also times when the daughter doesn't ever want to return, because she knows her father will not allow the drugs and the parties in his house, and she doesn't think she can live without them anymore. She justifies them as fun, and thinks her father is being too harsh by not allowing these behaviors. But when she wakes up the next morning, and sees and feels the conditions she has allowed herself to live in, and the person she has become, she often wishes she could go back home where she had an amazing life. She remembers what it was like to be loved and taken care of. Her father is ready and waiting for his daughter to turn back to him at any time. He knocks on the door and calls and messages his daughter, hoping that one day she will answer.

This is how God feels when we reject Him. He made us. He gave us everything we have ever needed, all of the minerals, plants and animals to sustain us, providing material for clothing, shelter, and food. All of the sunlight, stars, moon, and forces that keep our planet habitable. Our breath. We are His sons and daughters, but instead of listening to Him, and following a few simple rules, we instead turn to idols. Other gods, other addictions, other things that provide us seeming joy, or comfort, or escape from some of the stresses of life. In reality those other "false gods" are destroying us. Like the loving father above, all God wants is for His children, every one of us, to come back to Him. To turn to Him as our help when we are experiencing trouble or grief, instead of these other deceptive things. But, also like the father in the above story, He cannot just force us to come back and live in His house. We have to be willing to listen to Him and allow Him back into our lives to help us.

Unfortunately, we are like the daughter in the story. Sometimes we are too ashamed of the things we have done. We are fearful we will never receive God's forgiveness. Other times we find ourselves at the opposite extreme of loving our addictions and idols so much, we become too afraid to give them up. Either way, our fears are keeping us from God's love. We have to trust and believe that our Father is ready to forgive us and wants us back in His house. We have to be ready to work on ourselves and relinquish those things that are destroying us so that we are able to have a solid relationship with Him. We cannot continue to run back to our destructive ways of life, looking to others to meet our needs, and then also expect God to work in our lives. We have to choose between following Him, or chasing the idols of this world, and we have to trust that the life He has to offer us is far better than the one we are currently living without Him.

The story is somewhat of a more modern variation of the story of the prodigal son from the Bible. In the same way the prodigal son (and the daughter in our story) must be willing to return to his father, we must be willing to pursue a relationship with our Father, God. This is scary for most of us. We are afraid of His wrath over the things we have done. We are afraid of looking foolish in front of our friends and family, or we feel shame and are uncertain of His love for us. Sometimes we are worried we will have to give up some of our favorite things. All I can say is that if you start your pursuit, just take the first steps, you will be surprised at what you learn and experience. One thing I know for sure, is that no matter what you have done, no matter how bad you think you are, God still loves you. You are not too far gone, His love and mercy will find you wherever you are. When you finally do turn back and pursue Him, don't be afraid. He will come running joyfully to meet you!

God repeatedly warns the people of Israel that they will turn away from Him to worship false idols, and of course, they repeatedly do. When they turn away and pray to false idols for help, they suffer, because those false idols cannot protect them and help them like He does. He cannot provide for His children if they are choosing to follow other gods instead of Him. But He also tells them they can return to Him, and when they do, He will be ready to help them again. One example can be found in Deuteronomy 4 verses 28-31, "There you will serve gods, the work of men's hands, wood and stone, which neither see, nor hear, nor eat, nor smell. But from there you shall seek Yahweh your God, and you will find him when you search after him with all your heart and with all your soul. When you are in oppression, and all these things have come on you, in the latter days you shall return to Yahweh your God and listen to his voice. For Yahweh your God is a merciful God."

Knowing God isn't just about throwing a cross around your neck, attending church every Sunday, and posting memes on social media. This book, as well as the remaining books in this series, are attempts to push you as you walk along the pathway to a powerful relationship with God, to encourage you as you stumble along the way, and to help you truly recognize what is at stake. God loves you, no matter what. God is calling out to you to turn toward Him, and He wants you to **pursue Him like He is pursuing you**.

NOTES

2
RECOGNITION OF SIN

"He who conceals his sins doesn't prosper, but whoever confesses and renounces them finds mercy."
  - Proverbs 28:13

"What shall we say then? Is the law sin? May it never be! However, I wouldn't have known sin except through the law. For I wouldn't have known coveting unless the law had said, "You shall not covet."
  - Romans 7:7

Have you ever asked yourself, do you know for sure whether or not you will get into Heaven? How certain are you, and is there a way you can be sure? In my experience, many people are under the impression that, in order to get into Heaven, you must be a good person. So the next logical question would be, are you a good person? My guess is that many of you would instantly answer, "yes", or "pretty much", while a few of you are already starting to feel a little uncertain about your level of "goodness". Some of us base our goodness on a balance scale, hoping that we have done plenty of good things, and that the bad things we may have done are infrequent and minor enough to be outweighed by the good. Perhaps we think it is like a math equation, Number of Good Acts - Number of Bad Acts = Heaven/Hell, and we hope our badness will be canceled out by our overall goodness, thereby ending up with a positive answer to our math problem. On the other hand, some of us may fear that our difference will be a negative number, and worry there is no hope.

But, if it is in fact the case that only the "good" people can get into Heaven, then I have a follow-up question. I really don't want to rely on merely hoping I can get to Heaven, I want to know for sure. Am I good enough? Do my good acts outweigh the bad? How does my personal equation work out? In order to know that, we first have to define what exactly it means to be a good person. What criteria do I have to meet? Since we are talking about what it means to be good enough for the purposes of getting into Heaven, it makes sense that we should look to the Bible for that definition. God says we must follow His Commandments. So, while there are other laws included in the Bible, let's just start with what is generally referred to as the Ten Commandments, from Deuteronomy 5:6-21:

1. I am Yahweh your God, who brought you out of the land of Egypt, out of the house of bondage. You shall have no other gods before me.

2. You shall not make a carved image for yourself—any likeness of what is in heaven above, or what is in the earth beneath, or that is in the water under the earth. You shall not bow yourself down to them, nor serve them, for I, Yahweh your God, am a jealous God, visiting the iniquity of the

fathers on the children and on the third and on the fourth generation of those who hate me and showing loving kindness to thousands of those who love me and keep my commandments.

3. You shall not misuse the name of Yahweh your God; for Yahweh will not hold him guiltless who misuses his name.

4. Observe the Sabbath day, to keep it holy, as Yahweh your God commanded you. You shall labor six days, and do all your work; but the seventh day is a Sabbath to Yahweh your God, in which you shall not do any work— neither you, nor your son, nor your daughter, nor your male servant, nor your female servant, nor your ox, nor your donkey, nor any of your livestock, nor your stranger who is within your gates; that your male servant and your female servant may rest as well as you. You shall remember that you were a servant in the land of Egypt, and Yahweh your God brought you out of there by a mighty hand and by an outstretched

arm. Therefore Yahweh your God commanded you to keep the Sabbath day.

5. Honor your father and your mother, as Yahweh your God commanded you, that your days may be long and that it may go well with you in the land which Yahweh your God gives you.
6. You shall not murder.
7. You shall not commit adultery.
8. You shall not steal.
9. You shall not give false testimony against your neighbor.
10. You shall not covet your neighbor's wife. Neither shall you desire your neighbor's house, his field, or his male servant, or his female servant, his ox, or his donkey, or anything that is your neighbor's.

Now that we have reviewed them, let's judge our own goodness against them. Ask yourself if you have ever broken any of them at any time in your life. I will never know your answers, and God already knows them, so please feel free to be honest with yourself as you answer. Have you ever told a lie in your life, no matter how innocent? Have you ever stolen anything at all, or charged someone too much for something, no matter how small of a monetary amount it was? Have you ever had lustful thoughts? Have you ever had your fortune told, your chakras aligned, relied on your horoscope, or had symbols of other religious deities in your home or on your body? Have you ever sworn using God's name? Have you ever hated someone or hurt someone out of anger? Have you ever been jealous of someone's money, possessions, or life?

I'm fairly certain that the majority of you reading this book are answering most, if not all, of these questions with a resounding "yes". So if you are guilty of any one, or all of these things, then that makes you guilty of violating God's law, the Ten Commandments. Violating just one Commandment puts you in danger. If you are thinking smugly that you have never broken any of these Commandments, then you probably just told a lie, and might also have issues of pride to work on! Even worse, some, if not all, of these are "thought crimes", so if you have ever just wished to yourself that you had a fancier car like your boss, then you are guilty. I unfortunately know that I have done all of these things at one point or another. By all outward appearances, however, I am a good person. I have a respectable job, and a nice family. I volunteer my time and money, and behave in a way that is generally acceptable in my community. My mistakes were relatively small and fixable in the eyes of society. But in reality, and in God's eyes, I was a lying, cheating, manipulating, money-hungry, angry blasphemer, to say the least. Decidedly NOT a good person according to these commands.

Surely, we think, a just and forgiving God wouldn't send us to hell based on the few little things we have done wrong in our lives. Thinking envious thoughts shouldn't condem us to burn for eternity. Our little white lies shouldn't damn us to hell. We try to justify our behavior, by saying it isn't as bad as what *other* people do. After all, there are serial killers, rapists, and pedophiles, for goodness sakes. People whom we consider truly depraved, maybe even downright evil. We think we are obviously much better than them; we have never done anything remotely like that. If salvation is based on a balance scale, our badness could not possibly weigh nearly as much as theirs does! But, if you haven't finished reading the Bible yet, here's a quick spoiler: those *other* people have as much chance of receiving salvation as you or I do! Many people in prison and rehab have repented and turned to the Lord. So how exactly does that work? We think to ourselves that we are definitely great people when compared to those *others*, so if they can receive salvation, we should have no problem!

Not so fast. You see, in order to follow Jesus, He tells us we must first admit that we are sinners and acknowledge our sins. We cannot rely on believing that we are saved merely because we think we are not as bad as someone else. In Luke 18:9-14, Jesus warns us of the dangers of assuming that we are justified because we are better than those *others*:

> He also spoke this parable to certain people who were convinced of their own righteousness, and who despised all others: "Two men went up into the temple to pray; one was a Pharisee, and the other was a tax collector. The Pharisee stood and prayed by himself like this: 'God, I thank you that I am not like the rest of men: extortionists, unrighteous, adulterers, or even like this tax collector. I fast twice a week. I give tithes of all that I get.' But the tax collector, standing far away,

wouldn't even lift up his eyes to heaven, but beat his breast, saying, 'God, be merciful to me, a sinner!' I tell you, this man went down to his house justified rather than the other; for everyone who exalts himself will be humbled, but he who humbles himself will be exalted."

In a sinner's prayer, we typically ask to be forgiven of all of our sins. It would be pretty strange to ask for forgiveness from someone without first admitting we did something wrong. If we do not believe we have done anything wrong, why would we need to ask Him to forgive us? Those *others*, as they began their pursuit of God's Kingdom, had to first agree with and admit to Him that the things they did were wrong. This makes sense to us, doesn't it? I mean murder and the other things they did are horrific crimes, so of course they should, at the very least, have to realize and admit that they were wrong. But, obviously, we think to ourselves, "I have never done anything *that* bad. I'm basically a good person...."

.....a good person who has likely just admitted to breaking God's law by being a liar or a thief? As humans, we have this natural tendency to hide our flaws from the rest of the world, and even from ourselves. We make every excuse to justify our own sinful behaviors. We believe that certain lies are OK. We overlook them because they're just about innocent little things, and everyone does it. While hanging out shopping with a friend we say things like, "I'm going to sneak this brand new (purse, fish, tool) into the house so my spouse doesn't notice it. I'll just say that we always had it, if they even ask about it in the first place." Everyone chuckles and we assume it's harmless, normal, acceptable behavior. Or we scream, flip off, tailgate, and honk at other drivers going too slow in the fast lane, and brake check anyone who dares to drive too close to us. But that's normal, right? Most people do it, and everyone should learn how to drive! We overindulge in food, alcohol, electronic devices, and/or drugs because it seems fun and relaxing, and we believe it is what we deserve after a stressful day. We take more than our share of freebies, because we might as well grab as much as we can. Or we watch films with nudity and sex, and joke about which celebrities we wish we could be with. Society, our culture, tells us that all of these behaviors are ok, or at worst, minor everyday little vices, so why does God say they are not?

Because, as it turns out, none of these sinful behaviors are actually harmless. The constant sneaky purchases are pushing the family further and further into debt, and bringing added stress to the home, not to mention the wedge of distrust that each little lie hammers into the marriage. Feeling like you have to hide purchases from your spouse might be a sign of a larger problem that you are not dealing with. Road rage is clearly harmful to the person doing the yelling, as they risk raising their blood pressure and stress level over something that realistically only had a minor effect on the length of their commute. And who knows what was going on in that other driver's life at that moment? Perhaps they are on their way to work all night after leaving their sick child at the hospital, and now they have you flipping them off and honking at them, as if their day wasn't bad enough. Our overindulgences hurt our health, and cost us time and money. They usually cause more damage to our mental well-being than stress-relief overall, but we prefer to blame our problems on everything but our own behavior. When we take more than we need, it means there might not be enough for everyone else, and we wind up with more than we can realistically use. Our seemingly silly celebrity worship subconsciously leads to unrealistic expectations, which cause tiny undercurrents of resentment about our own lives and partners. Everything we do affects those around us and/or ourselves in some way.

We need to raise our awareness of how the small things we do have a ripple effect. This can be extremely difficult to accept and understand, especially when we try to do it on our own. Our natural instinct is to make excuses for our sinful behavior. We attempt to justify what we have done because it was twenty years ago, or we just had the thought, but never acted on it. We try to hide our sinful nature from God, but we forget that He is the one who created us. He knows that we are sinful people. He knows everything we do, we cannot hide from Him. He gave us the laws and commandments to shine a spotlight on all of the ways we are drawn to, and commit, evil. By explicitly telling us that certain things are wrong, He is trying to teach us not to do those things, but for whatever reason, we all choose to go ahead and do them anyway. The whole point of those laws was to show us that we are all guilty of something, and are all in need of His salvation. We could never be good enough to save ourselves because we have all already broken the laws. The crimes have been committed.

There is no shortage of religious people ready and willing to tell us what is sinful. I often hear pastors preaching constantly about how awful things like homosexuality, drug abuse, and abortion are. It would lead one to believe that these are some of the biggest problems facing their own parishioners, and therefore they need ample teaching on those topics. While it is certainly important to teach the whole Bible, and a sin is a sin, what might be of greater use to their parishioners would be to teach about the particular types of sin that impact their own daily lives. Things like gossip, rage, selfishness, lust, greed, and judgment are more likely to be the sins that they are grappling with. Learning how even some of their 'minor' transgressions are problematic could open up their hearts to a more productive relationship with the Lord. In addition, by talking directly about the very sins the members of the congregation are battling, the pastor is demonstrating that just because something is sinful, does not mean that we must demonize the people who commit those sins. We can love the person, as God commands, and help them to build their own relationship with God. Then *He* will help them work through their sins.

Everyone wants to call out the general sins of society, but no one wants to examine their own. In my experience, teaching about the sins of other people, while ignoring our own sins, most often leads to exclusionary practices, and feelings of superiority, rather than introspection. If, for instance, we spend most of our time teaching the children in the church youth group that homosexuality is bad, but rarely go into detail about what a lie is, or how to be humble and not envious, we risk creating little monsters who go around bullying kids who are different, instead of followers of Christ who know that He can save anyone from any sin.

By doing this, we set our children up for failure, because God does not want His people preventing others from finding Him. In fact, we are called to do the opposite and lead people to Jesus. How can you lead someone to Jesus, and help them stop their sinful behavior, if you make them feel unwelcome in the places where His gospel is taught? Their sins are no greater or worse than your sins or my sins. Thankfully, it seems like more and more churches are rejecting the rituals and judgment wrapped up in religion, in favor of focusing only on the Bible. Recognizing our own sins is crucial, because it makes us aware that we have no right to act superior, or to prevent anyone else from hearing God's word. In order to bring others to the foot of the cross, we have to relate to their stories, by admitting they are a lot like our own. If Jesus can save us, He can save them too. If we each looked at church as a place where we could spend time working with God on our own shortcomings, and supporting others on their journeys, the church would be much stronger.

Recognizing our own sins is not an easy task to accomplish. It starts off fine at first; we might recall some of our more obvious and outrageous behaviors, and we understand why they were wrong. But we still fall into the trap of justifying our smaller sins, especially the ones in our minds. For example, we do not necessarily think of our behavior as sinful when someone else starts an argument and we respond with our own angry outbursts. God wants better for us though, and if we allow Him to work on us, we will soon be able to see our behaviors the way He does, and desire to change. As you struggle, you will come to realize you are not capable of working through this process by yourself, and being successful at it. You will likely not truly comprehend the depths of your sinfulness unless you ask for help. In a later chapter, we will focus more on how God provides us the help we need as we go through this process, but here is a quick preview. One of the most important parts of effective change in your life will be the pursuit of, and eventual reliance upon, your relationship with Him. Essential to that is the gift He gave us - the ability to have His Holy Spirit fill our hearts. As you are considering all of your potentially sinful behaviors and thoughts, talk to Him. Ask His Holy Spirit to take an inventory of your mind, heart, and soul. Allow Him to make you aware of your sins, and any harm you have caused yourself or others. You might find yourself surprised at what pops up in your memory!

What God has shown me on my journey, is that we should define what is sinful as *anything that takes us away from God*. What turns me away from His purpose for me? Anything that distracts me from following Him, or causes feelings of shame in me is sinful. Anything I feel like I have to hide from Him or feel guilt over. I can learn and know if something I am doing is sinful by talking to God and building my relationship with Him. If I listen to Him, and allow Him to teach me through His Holy Spirit, then I can begin to understand my own sins, and the changes I must make. Jesus only died for the sinners. This is because a) we are all sinners and b) because it is only by agreeing that what we have done is sinful, and admitting that we have been sinners, that we are able to follow through with repentance of those sins, and to understand our need for His salvation.

Notes

3

THE CONSEQUENCES
OF SIN

"You have heard that it was said to the ancient ones, 'You shall not murder;' and 'Whoever murders will be in danger of the judgment.' But I tell you that everyone who is angry with his brother without a cause will be in danger of the judgment. Whoever says to his brother, 'Raca!' will be in danger of the council. Whoever says, 'You fool!' will be in danger of the fire of Gehenna.

...

You have heard that it was said, 'You shall not commit adultery;' but I tell you that everyone who gazes at a woman to lust after her has committed adultery with her already in his heart."

- Jesus (Matthew 5:21-22 and 27-28)

When I was growing up, most of my friends went to the same type of church. They prayed the rosary, they had catechism classes after school, and they confessed their sins to a priest. Having been raised in a different denomination, I did not do any of those things. I was a little jealous that they had all of these rituals they knew that I didn't, but I was also extremely thankful that my family's church did not require priestly confession. The thought of having to tell some grown man about every lie I told, or every fight I had with my siblings just seemed embarrassing and terrifying. When my friends would talk about what they did during confession, they would tell me that after they confessed their sins to the priest, he would tell them to apologize, not to do it again, and then prescribe a certain number and kind of prayer for them to say as resolution. As a child, the whole thing seemed strange to me, and I guess I assumed if they said seven Hail Mary prayers, that would serve as the punishment for whatever sins they had committed. Sort of like writing lines if you misbehaved in class.

Of course, my understanding back then was limited, and I did not know all of the nuances and reasons behind each tradition. I still admit I am not familiar with all of the justifications for the many religious rituals among the various denominations, however, now that I am an adult, I do find that I generally agree with my childhood self. For one, I have read the entire Bible, and still read it every day, and I cannot find anything that says praying a Hail Mary on a rosary will rectify anyone's sins. In addition, Mary, the mother of Jesus, is not God. She was human like the rest of us, faithfully following orders. She did an outstanding job doing what God asked her to do, but Jesus did not pray to her. He prayed to His Father, God. Lastly, Mary is dead. In Isaiah 8:19 we are cautioned to talk to God, not the dead, "When they tell you, 'Consult with those who have familiar spirits and with the wizards, who chirp and who mutter,' shouldn't a people consult with their God? Should they consult the dead on behalf of the living?" Praying to a dead person to intercede for you with God seems like adding an unnecessary step, since you can now pray directly to God yourself. It is absolutely true that intercessory prayer (praying to God for the needs of others) is very powerful, but it makes sense when done by the living who are praying to the Lord, and are increasing the volume of your own cries to Heaven, or praying for you when you are incapacitated. Praying *to* anyone other than the Lord does not seem to fit with what I read in the Bible, and sounds a lot like idolatry.

Be careful about just blindly following the dogma and traditions of any particular church or denomination, because sometimes you might find out later that they are outside of God's word. God's judgment, the punishment for our sins, and our salvation are not fulfilled by a rosary, a prayer to a saint, or confession to a priest. You don't want to wait, as you never know when your day will come, but people can even be saved on their deathbeds as long as they fully return to God, and confess and repent of their sins. Just like the thief who was crucified next to Christ, you do not need any special ceremonies to return to God. There is no perfect religion, church, or group, because they are all run by imperfect humans. Therefore, it is imperative that we be mindful to learn God's word for ourselves and follow Him and Him alone.

As far as confession goes, I have discovered that confessing my sins is not as bad as I thought it would be. Though I was once terrified to admit any of my sins to anyone, it became so much easier to do so the more I learned and understood about God's mercy. It is true that one of the consequences of our sins is that we must acknowledge and confess them, but I cannot find anything that says we must confess our sins to any particular person. We must certainly confess our sins to God, because we must acknowledge they were wrong and turn away from them. We are also told in James 5:16, "Confess your sins to one another and pray for one another, that you may be healed. The insistent prayer of a righteous person is powerfully effective." Which means that we should confess our sins to other people when our confessions are needed to help each other heal.

One example would be confessing to those whom you have sinned against, such as returning something you took from someone, or apologizing for a lie that you told. Just like the wealthy tax collector, Zacchaeus, did in Luke 19, verse 8, "Zacchaeus stood and said to the Lord, "Behold, Lord, half of my goods I give to the poor. If I have wrongfully exacted anything of anyone, I restore four times as much." If there is a way we can right a wrong, we should make the effort to do so. This is not easy to do at all, but if you enlist God's help and start with a less difficult apology first, it may build your confidence. One of the more immediate consequences of our sins is that, as they are revealed to us as sin, we are then called upon to repent and, if possible, make amends for the harm we have caused. Personally speaking, God has convinced me to apologize to people, even when I initially thought I wasn't the one who needed to apologize. He has required me to pay back more than five times the amount of some money that I stole, even though it had been many years ago and I had basically forgotten about it. When He did bring it to my attention, I realized that I had been trying to justify my actions in my mind as something other than theft. God is relentless and He will root out all of those areas where you need to see the error of your ways. He will bring them to light and ask you to repent and make them right. You will probably be nervous about this, or sometimes unsure of why you need to make amends, but if you trust Him and learn from what He is teaching you, this process will heal both you, and the people you have hurt in the past.

An additional reason we must confess our sins is to make us humble, and force us to recognize our need for salvation and mercy. No one can fix a problem if they are not aware of it. When you start to realize just how many mistakes you have made in your lifetime, it has a way of putting things in perspective. If we already think we are good enough to go to Heaven, then we won't have much need to build a relationship with the Lord, and be cleansed of our sins. If however, we see ourselves as sinful as we truly are, we become desperate to stop our sinful behaviors. We find ourselves crying out for His mercy. Because, as we will soon discuss, our only means of salvation is through Him.

Another reason for confessing our sins to one another, is to help everyone else find their way, so they can be spiritually healed of their sins. As you walk on your journey with God, you will find yourself telling others about your path. Confessing your sins can help them understand God's mercy and see a ray of hope for forgiveness of their own sins. Many people are afraid of going to church, joking that the ceiling would cave in if they walked through the doors because they are such terrible sinners. However, if we are all just willing to be honest with each other, they will see that we all have problems, they do not have to be afraid. We all fall far short of adhering to these Commandments. None of us are free from sin. If the church didn't cave in when I walked in, it won't when you do either. We cannot come to someone in need of God's love, and pretend to be superior to them, simply because our sins might be a little more socially acceptable, or because we feel like we are further along on the path. We need to invite them in and make them feel at ease, by talking with them about how we still found God, despite our own shortcomings. We need to feel safe being open about the wrong things we have done, and how God helped us learn to do better. We need to pray for them consistently, that they too will find God.

In a later chapter we will talk about forgiveness and judgment, because confessing to others that we are sinners also makes it that much more difficult to judge them. Hopefully, if you did confess your sins to a pastor, their response would be one of compassion, guiding you to repentance and forgiveness. Confession is good for the soul. Ultimately, even if there was no one left on this planet for you to make amends with or to confess your sins to, you would still have to deal with God, and His judgment, and that should concern you far more than talking about your sins with any of the people around you!

On the flip side, we also must be careful not to go too far to the point where we are glorifying our sins. We have all either talked, or heard people talk, about the mistakes we made in our younger years, and it often sounds like we are bragging about them. When we sit around with our friends recalling the time we broke into our parents' liquor cabinet and drank so much we had to fill the bottle with tea to hide it, we often laugh and try to top one another's stories. This is not repentance. Things like disrespecting our parents, stealing, and lying are not something to boast about. If we think they are something to take pride in, or a funny story to impress our friends with, then we are failing to recognize that they were wrong. As you may know, or will learn, Jesus paid a very high price for all of our sins, and when we glorify them, we essentially become part of the crowd spitting at Him while He was being tortured to death.

And please don't go around constantly talking about how unworthy and awful you are. Yes, it is probably true, but God does not want us to live ashamed and hidden away. As you will soon read, God is merciful and forgives our sinfulness, but if we continue to wallow in self-pity, we are no better off. He doesn't want us to punish ourselves over and over again because we made these mistakes; He wants us to learn to do better and to listen to His voice. He wants us to see our mistakes as stepping stones on the path to finding Him, not as an eternal weight on our shoulders. In the story about the loving father, if his daughter does follow her father's plan, and returns home restored to her healthy lifestyle, should she grovel at her father's feet daily, crying, apologizing, and begging for mercy? Spend her days laying in bed, depressed about what a bad daughter she has been? Her father has already shown that he loves her, has helped her to clean up her life, and allowed her back in the house. If the daughter spends all day, every day, feeling guilty and ashamed, and reliving her mistakes over and over again, she will be far more susceptible to return to the temptations that led her astray in the first place, searching for comfort. In addition, the father's gift of help for the daughter is practically useless if the daughter doesn't undertake to have a better quality of life from that point forward. Much more preferable would be for the daughter to show remorse, apologize, clean up her act, and then get to work living the best life she can as a sign of gratitude to her father. If she does that, it will make it worth the sacrifices of worry, time, and money it took for the father to pull his daughter out of that bottomless pit. Just like the daughter, we must learn not to allow our sins to define our lives. Listen to God. Allow His Holy Spirit to heal you and fill you with peace, love, and joy instead of worry, grief, and shame. Clean up your act with His help and begin to live your life for Him.

So if confession of our sins is part of our earthly responsibility, how does that affect God's eternal judgment? It seems like somewhat of a natural, earthly consequence that if we sin, we must confess and make amends, but there must be more to it. What are the eternal consequences? What happens to those of us who violate God's commandments? What is the penalty we have to pay? Regrettably, the punishment for our sins is death. To explain, allow me to briefly review a bit of backstory.

Even if you have not read the Bible yet, you probably have at least a passing familiarity with Adam and Eve. When God created humans, he meant for us to be innocent, not ever knowing what evil was. The animals were the same, coexisting peacefully together. Neither humans nor animals ate flesh, as God gave the plants for food. We were supposed to be able to live in His perfect garden forever, walking with Him, unaware of evil. To protect people from learning about evil, God instructed Adam that they could have and eat anything from the garden, except for the fruit from the Tree of Knowledge of Good and Evil. If they disobeyed Him and touched or ate from that tree, God told Adam they would die. The serpent soon tempted Eve to eat the delicious fruit, by telling her that she would not die, but that she would have the knowledge of God. Then she tempted Adam to directly disobey God's command to Him. This was pivotal. Adam was faced with two choices. Listen to God and don't eat the fruit, or listen to someone else and eat. Adam defied his Father, ignored his Creator's command, and chose to listen instead to a lowly serpent and Eve. This is the free-will everyone talks about. The choice Adam and Eve made, and the choice we all make when we decide to follow something other than God, is done of our own free will.

Of course Adam and Eve did not immediately die when they took a bite, so this seems confusing. Was God wrong or lying when he said they would die? Absolutely not. For one, God wasn't just talking about a physical death, He was referring to our spiritual death. By choosing the serpent instead of God, Adam and Eve, and, by extension, all of us, were immediately cast out of paradise, cut off from a relationship with God. We became cursed to suffer and have pain in life, instead of spending an eternal life in the garden, in a good relationship with Him. Furthermore, if we do not return to God and allow Him to free us from our sinfulness, we will spend eternity suffering in spiritual death instead of life. In addition, humans were never meant to physically die. There was another tree in the garden, the Tree of Life. God knew that if Adam and Eve ate from the Tree of Life while they were in their fallen state of knowing evil, they would live forever, and so would the evil. Therefore, God had to keep humanity out of the garden, so we would not have access to the Tree of Life until we are cleansed. Since we cannot currently eat from the Tree of Life and stay alive, we all must face death, just as Adam and Eve eventually did.

The choice to listen to someone other than God was the sin that took humanity out of a strong relationship with Him, and left us vulnerable to evil temptations. We all now know and do evil, and our penalty for committing those violations against God, by lying, stealing, lusting, and allowing false gods to rule our life, is both physical and spiritual death. You may not yet fully realize it, but this is a hefty penalty, a huge cost to bear. We can get a glimpse through what Jesus described, as quoted in Luke 16:22-25:

> The beggar died, and he was carried away by the angels to Abraham's bosom. The rich man also died and was buried. In Hades, he lifted up his eyes, being in torment, and saw Abraham far off, and Lazarus at his bosom. He cried and said, 'Father Abraham, have mercy on me, and send Lazarus, that he may dip the tip of his finger in water and cool my tongue! For I am in anguish in this flame.'
> "But Abraham said, 'Son, remember that you, in your lifetime, received your good things, and Lazarus, in the same way, bad things. But here he is now comforted and you are in anguish.'

Ever since that original sin of Adam and Eve, we have been left out in this world to be tempted by darkness, yet feeling this yearning for God that we didn't even know was missing in our souls. If we do not listen to God calling out to us and turn back to Him, we are in danger of this fate of death.

After reading the previous chapter, you have probably realized that you have committed at least one or two sins in your life. We can stop putting all of the blame on Adam and Eve and accept that we, too, are guilty. We can come to terms with having to face this spiritual and physical death penalty. It is scary to accept this, but it is a crucial step, not because I *want* you to be a sinner, or to face this penalty, but because it is extremely important that you honestly admit that you have sinned. Unlike a district courtroom where your attorney might advise you to plead not-guilty, in God's court, the only path to redemption involves admitting you did wrong. Therefore, since you and I have sinned against God, we are guilty and deserving of the penalty of spiritual death. We have to come to terms with that fact and admit that what we did was wrong so that we can move forward.

I know it sounds terrifying to realize that by admitting we have ever told a lie, we have just essentially received the death penalty. Some of you may even be feeling quite despondent that your sins are too numerous or too awful for you to be saved, but you are going to have to trust God here. He says your soul is still worth saving, and He wants you back. He promises you that He has always had a plan to help you escape the death penalty. The even better news is that He also wants to set you free completely! So how does this all work?

Similar to the laws of any given country, when someone is found guilty of breaking the law, they receive some sort of punishment. Some crimes receive fines or restitution, some receive prison time or probation, and the most serious crimes often receive corporal punishment. Many places subject certain criminals to the death penalty, in some countries more than others. In this case, the penalty for violating any of the Commandments is death.

This is it. You have admitted your guilt, and the punishment for your crimes is death. You are currently on death row, so to speak. Your execution could come at any moment. You have one last hearing before the judge who will decide your fate. Picture yourself standing in front of the court, moments away from a decision on your life. Will you be sent to your death or pardoned and set free? You could try to plead your case and explain all of your excuses and reasons for your behavior, blaming it on everyone and everything else. You could try to pretend like you didn't do anything wrong, because millions of other people have done the same crime. You could try to illustrate and rationalize that what you did wasn't that bad. Or you could accept responsibility, repent of your crimes, and throw yourself at the mercy of the court. Your answer might depend on who the judge was.

So let's picture that same scenario, but instead of picturing yourself in an earthly courtroom, imagine your judge is the Most High God and it is the day of your own judgment. You may have a guess about what God's mercy looks like, but for now, my goal is to try to paint the picture for you of just how desperate the situation is. The thought of standing all alone in front of any human courtroom is nerve-wracking enough for most of us, so we gather our evidence, prepare our arguments, and often hire an attorney to represent us. Strangely though, very few of us are purposefully preparing for our final spiritual judgment day. We just sort of hope that things will work out for the best, and we make up our own ideas about who God is, but few of us really plan ahead. We might look up all of the laws and policies that apply to our small claims case about our neighbor's tree, but completely ignore the laws that apply to God's spiritual judgment of our souls. Yet, if you try to put yourself in the position of what it would genuinely feel like to stand before God, have your deepest, darkest secrets revealed, and face accusations about your life, you might find the thought shakes you. Hopefully that feeling rouses you into action to begin preparations urgently. Because, let's be honest, you could die today and be summoned to your final judgment. You have no idea how much time you have to prepare for that hearing, are you ready?

Perhaps, as noted previously, you think you can save yourself from this penalty just by doing more good things than bad things. If so, you are mistaken. First of all, it is impossible for us to live a sin-free life apart from God, so every day you will likely end up committing several sins, often without even realizing it. Every time you fuss over how you look in your jeans and how your hair and makeup look, every time you think about what a pain your annoying coworker is. Every time you swear in anger using God's name. Every time you get depressed and/or enraged over the latest political distractions. Every time you charge too much for the merchandise you sell, or cheat someone in a deal, you are adding more accusers at your hearing, and more evidence against you. The negative side of your balance scale gets heavier every day.

And if we are balancing your scale or tallying your equation, let's go ahead and figure out what good works you are doing that you believe will make up for and outweigh all of these 'minor' transgressions. What are your good deeds? Rounding up your change for some random charity at the checkout lane? Volunteering once a month at the soup kitchen? Singing at the church every Sunday and leading the PTA on Tuesday? Joining the chain of folks, "paying it forward" at your local coffee shop drive-through? Donating all of your old clothes/Knick knacks/TV's to the thrift shop or donation bin? Yay! Don't get me wrong, those things are all great and they can be very helpful and kind, but can we please be realistic? None of these require much effort or sacrifice on your part, and often we do these things mainly to satisfy our own ego, rather than out of a selfless desire to actually help someone in need.

If you were the judge, would you let a several-times guilty criminal off the hook if they came up to you with a bit of a holier-than-thou attitude, and showing no real signs of remorse? If they just made a bunch of blame-shifting excuses for their crimes, and tried to downplay them? Then, as if to top it off, they had the nerve to try to justify the bad things they did by saying they always tip their service people extremely well, and donate blood at least once a year? Of course you wouldn't. You would at the very least want the criminal to admit their responsibility in the crimes and to own up to their behavior. Then you would want to see evidence that they understand that what they did was wrong, and they agree that they should not, and will not, do it anymore. And truly, most of us would want to see the criminal show remorse and repentance for what they did. To see them apologize to those who were hurt by their actions, to pay for any damages that were done, and to experience regret for what they did, so that you can be confident that they will not commit those crimes again if you set them free. Why do we think God should require anything less of us?

If we are being completely honest, most of us aren't even doing that many "good works" in an average week anyway. On a typical day, we go to work, pick up the kids and run to extracurricular activities, come home, eat, and clean up after ourselves, then complain about all of the work we had to do. We sit in bed and post memes about how we deserve a cocktail on the beach or a day of pampering, when the truth is, most of us haven't done much of anything on any given day to deserve a reward. We work to pay for the things we need and want to buy. We take care of our own needs, and sometimes our family's needs, by doing basic things like cooking, shopping, eating, and cleaning, and we complain about having to do that. We rarely go out of our way to help others, and when we do, we tend to make a big deal out of it, posting about our good deeds on social media. Do you really feel you deserve rewards simply for doing what is expected of you? If I want to eat, it is reasonable to expect that I have to do something to get the food: earn money to purchase, or plant and harvest the food, and prepare it. If I want shelter, it is reasonable to expect that I should work to either build, or pay for, the kind of shelter I choose to live in. If I have children, it is reasonable that I should work to provide the care they need. Even the wild animals work to provide their food and daily needs, and to take care of their young. We need to stop acting like these things are such a burden, perhaps then we will stop feeling so resentful and overwhelmed. And all of the extra things we spend our time on, the things that aren't necessary for life, such as clubs, sports, and working overtime to buy fancier things? Those are choices each of us make. God never says our kids have to be signed up for soccer and art camp in order for us to be saved. God never says we deserve to live in a 4000 square foot home with several luxury vehicles, a manicured lawn, and brand name clothes. We put those expectations on ourselves, or allow society to put them on us. We do not deserve a reward because we choose to run ourselves ragged, just to accumulate material possessions and the admiration of others. This drive to be overworked, and to do more, is neglecting what is important, and certainly does not constitute a good work deserving of releasing you from the death penalty. In fact, if it means you are too busy and too tired to read the Bible and spend time with the Lord, your drive has become a false idol. If you were counting on the scale tipping in your favor, I wouldn't.

Maybe you recognize that you have sinned, but you think you can avoid the death penalty by explaining why it isn't your fault. You think that you are not guilty because someone else made you sin. Unfortunately, the excuse many schoolchildren try to use (Johnny told me to do it!) didn't work too well for Adam or Eve, and it won't work for you either. Adam blamed his eating of the forbidden fruit on Eve, Eve blamed hers on the serpent, and all three of them had to pay the price. We have to be able to really internally admit that what *we* did was wrong, regardless of any outside influence or role someone else may have played. We have to stop making excuses for all of our negative behaviors and come to terms with our own role, rather than blaming others for provoking us. When someone starts a fight with us, God wants us to be the bigger person and, as Jesus teaches us, to turn the other cheek to them, so to speak. We are not supposed to seek our own vengeance. We also have to understand the harms we have caused and freely and honestly repent, so that we are careful never to do those things again.

I hope by now, you are starting to see that attempting to save yourself is looking pretty futile. If you stood in court and tried to make these arguments to a judge, they probably would not go over very well. This same thinking applies to you, and to all of us, in God's courtroom, because we are all guilty of so many crimes. Getting a criminal set free from death row isn't generally the easiest thing in the world. In an earthly trial, you would want the best attorney you could afford representing you, so you wouldn't have to go it alone. In the same way, confronting our sins, and dealing with the possibility of spiritual death is heavy stuff. If you try to do it alone, it will become too overwhelming. The more you delve into your lifestyle, the more transgressions you will start to recall. You may believe the voices telling you that you have done too many bad things to ever be worthy of being loved by God. This is why the sinner's prayer is important. We ask the Holy Spirit to come into our hearts. By inviting Him in, He is able to strengthen us when those voices start trying to lie to us. By inviting Him in, we are also allowing Him to dredge up all of our sins and bring them to our attention, so we can be cleansed of them, and remove them from our record. The Holy Spirit will also help you through this part of the process, and will be with you to support you when you start to feel the fear that is brought about by recalling your sins, and the fear of the death penalty you face.

In the next chapter, we will learn how we do not have to fear the day of our judgment. The main goal of this chapter was to help convince you of your need for

God to have mercy on you, and to save you. For you to realize that you are dependent on Him, and do not have the power to save yourself. I encourage you to pray and ask God to help you admit to your sins, to make you aware of them, and ask for guidance from the Holy Spirit. This is not a one day, one week, or even one year process, it will last your lifetime. I had over 40 years of sins to deal with when I first returned to God, and while He is working on me and making me better, I still add more to the list. If you continue to pray every time you find yourself drifting into negative behavior, I promise you that He will walk you through this, teach you about your weaknesses, and help you grow.

I often prayed something along these lines:

Father God, Please, I beg You, let Your Holy Spirit convict me of all of my sins. Show them to me and help me to learn the lessons I am supposed to learn. Please help me to see how my actions affect myself and others. Please help me to accept responsibility for my choices. I want to learn what You think is sinful God, and I want to learn why. I am sorry that I have hurt people with my actions, and I want to learn how to do better. Thank You for all You have given me.

Amen.

I still pray this type of prayer today. Once you start the process you eventually realize there are a lot of transgressions that can happen in a lifetime. There is never a better moment than now to get started. You never know when the jailers will come to collect you for your trial, so don't delay!

NOTES

4

GOD'S PLAN FOR SALVATION

"[F]or by grace you have been saved through faith, and that not of yourselves; it is the gift of God, not of works, that no one would boast."
-   Ephesians 2:8-9

"But if we walk in the light as he is in the light, we have fellowship with one another, and the blood of Jesus Christ his Son, cleanses us from all sin. If we say that we have no sin, we deceive ourselves, and the truth is not in us. If we confess our sins, he is faithful and righteous to forgive us the sins and to cleanse us from all unrighteousness. If we say that we haven't sinned, we make him a liar, and his word is not in us."
-   1 John 1:7-10

As we just learned, there is a really horrific penalty awaiting all sinners on the day of God's judgment. Yet here we all are, admitting to ourselves that we are guilty. We have accepted the fact that our sins are deserving of some type of punishment, and unfortunately for all of us, the punishment for breaking these laws is death. If I get caught driving 55 in a 45, I will get a ticket and will be subjected to the penalty of paying a fine. If I am found guilty of murder, I may get time in prison or even the death penalty. God sees everything I do, I have been caught breaking His laws, I have admitted my guilt, and I am subject to the death penalty. So what does that really mean? Aren't we all going to die someday? I thought God had a plan to save us?

You may be thinking, like I was, that this sounds like an epic problem! There was a law, I broke it, I'm guilty. I don't want to suffer spiritual death. I can't "go on the run" because God can find me anywhere, so what is the point if I am just going to suffer this spiritual death penalty? I learned I cannot save myself by doing good deeds or praying a rosary, so I could really use some good news right about now, because this sounds hopeless.

Back in the earlier biblical times, people used to burn unblemished sacrificial animals to atone for their sins. Does this mean I have to start doing that? I have a feeling I would be hauled away for animal cruelty!

Well, yes, the punishment for sins is death, therefore we need unblemished, innocent blood to be shed as the payment of death to atone for our sins, but NO, please don't start having animal sacrifices in your backyard. There is some Good, really Magnificent News! All of the work to save us has already been done! The sacrifice has already been made on our behalf! We all have a Savior! His name is Jesus Christ, Yeshua. He was sent to this earth as a sinless (unblemished) human, and His job while He was here was to spread the gospel, and explain God's word, then to save us all in order to fulfill God's ultimate plan. He did this by presenting Himself as the perfect, complete sacrifice for ALL of us and ALL of our sins. Because He had no faults, because He was sinless, His death and innocent blood could pay off the cost of each of our punishments so that we are all free to go. Instead of sacrificing billions of lambs, we only needed to sacrifice one pristine Lamb of God to set us free from the penalty of our sins.

Remember the scenario where you are the judge and you have the criminal in front of you? They have begged for mercy, have demonstrated their remorse for their crimes, and understand and admit their guilt. They are hoping to be pardoned. You firmly believe that they have changed, and in the interests of justice, you are convinced that the best course of action would be to allow them to go free. Unfortunately, your hands are tied. The law says they must pay for their crimes. After all, the damage was already done, and no amount of apologizing and good behavior can pay for the repairs. There are mandatory fines and restitution that must be paid, but the criminal has no means of paying. The fines are too high. Just when it looked like you would have to send the criminal to jail, someone else swoops in and pays for everything! As the judge, you can now ensure that justice prevails and pardon the former criminal, setting him free. He can go on to lead a productive life, contributing to society, instead of sitting in jail costing resources. This is essentially what Jesus did for us. We were the criminals.

He paid our debts by exchanging His life for ours, so that we could be set free. Even if you are struggling with your own political views on letting earthly criminals out of prison, spiritually we have all been blessed with a Savior whose desire is to see every one of us criminals unchained from our prisons. He knows our crimes, and He knows our heart and our repentance, and He wants us to accept His sacrifice and be set free.

How did this happen? Let me see if I can explain quickly, but please read this for yourself in the Bible to really appreciate the full picture. Jesus was sent here to live life as an ordinary human. He was born into lowly circumstances and worked hard all His life. He was Jewish and studied God's word until He could quote it by heart. He was later baptized by his cousin, John the Baptist. At that time, the Holy Spirit came upon Him, and He received spiritual gifts that would help Him as He completed God's mission for Him on Earth. He communicated daily with His Father, God, through prayer and fasting. He led a sinful, blameless life. After He was baptized, He began traveling, teaching others the word of God, and healing people. The religious and political leaders of the time eventually became troubled by what He was doing and tried to stop Him. When they couldn't, they ensured He was sentenced to death. He was tortured, beaten, humiliated, and worse. He chose to walk voluntarily to that torture and death, even though He knew it was coming. He did all of this because He loves us, and because He was obeying God's plan for Him to do so. His death was counted as payment for our sins, and they are washed away when we repent and turn to Him. Because He died blameless, He was able to get the keys to the cages that have kept all of our souls locked up away from God since the original sin of Adam and Eve. He has unlocked them all so that, when, and if, we make the choice, we are able to step out of our cages and follow His light. We can push our cage doors open and cry out for the help of our Lord and Savior. He says that if we call upon Him, He will guide us as we make our way home out of the darkness.

Wow, that is amazing. You mean, I did the crime, but Jesus took the guilt and accepted my punishment? Yes. He knew what was going to happen to Him. He asked if there was any other way, but in the end, He submitted to God's will. He followed through with what God asked Him to do and paid the ransom for us. And because of what He did, you and I have been set free. We no longer have to suffer spiritual death because of what He did by going to His execution to save us. Thank You Jesus! Yes, it really is true. Jesus has set each and every one of us free. We do not have to pay the penalty. But, there is a catch: in order to benefit from this gift of freedom, we have to claim it. We have to push open the unlocked door to the cages that are trapping our souls, climb out, and follow Him. We have to take advantage of our ability to listen to God and to pray to Him. We have to choose God with our whole mind, heart, and soul. We can no longer listen to the serpent and expect to live in God's garden.

And that is why being honest about our guilt and accepting that there is nothing we can do to save ourselves is so important. His plan is that we are not standing alone when we face our final judgment, but instead that we choose to be represented by His Son, our Savior, Jesus Christ, who has paid the price for us. You see, despite the fact that we have all fallen short and sinned, God still loves us and He wants to save us. Each one of us can have eternal life. Everyone will be gathered up and then He will sort us. God loves us so much that He created this way for us to be set free, but it is up to us to accept or reject His plan, and determine where we spend our eternal life. We now have the same choice as Adam and Eve did that day in the garden. We can accept God's offer of an eternal, rewarded life free from tears, with Him. Or we can listen to the serpents and choose the things of this world. However, if we reject His offer, we will spend eternity in torment, separated from God, suffering a second death.

Many times, when death is mentioned in the Bible, it has to do with our spiritual death more than our fleshly, earthly death. We worry so much about how our flesh will die, but not as much about our soul's eternal life. Since our life on Earth is short, but eternity is forever, we have to be careful that what we do now doesn't prevent us from reaching our Heavenly reward. Our sins keep us distant from God, our shame over our sins makes us hide from God, and our denial of our sinfulness makes us stop listening to the voice of God in our lives. If we do not understand the full weight and ramifications of our sins, then we will not appreciate our need for Jesus Christ, or comprehend the depths of God's mercy.

This, again, is where that whole "free will" concept comes into play. People often misunderstand this concept, and it leads to confusion about how evil is put into the world. God is good, but God gave each one of us the free will to choose God and his goodness, or to choose darkness and evil. Starting with that first choice in the Garden of Eden, darkness, through the devil and his fallen angels, has power on this earth. We are not in God's paradise anymore! As Jesus said in John 8:44, "You are of your father the devil, and you want to do the desires of your father. He was a murderer from the beginning, and doesn't stand in the truth, because there is no truth in him. When he speaks a lie, he speaks on his own; for he is a liar, and the father of lies." Just like the daughter in the story who listened to the lies of the other man, we all started listening to the lies of the devil. We have been convinced to do the work of the devil, and to turn away from what our own Father, God, calls us to do. We lie, hoard toilet paper, manipulate others, and shoplift. We gossip, complain about everything, and tear

80

people down. We road rage, cheat on our spouses, and drink too much. We spend hours at the gym or salon agonizing over how we look, and buy clothes, cars, and houses to impress others. We look down our noses at the scruffy person who walks into our church or place of business. We think we are so much better than drug addicts, or food addicts, or gambling addicts. And then we have the nerve to ask why there is evil on the Earth? Evil exists because we allow it. We listen to it. We promote it. We obey it. We practice it. We choose it. It is time to stop! God gives us the option to choose good, but we consistently choose evil.

This may come as a shock because we tend to consider ourselves to be mostly good, other than those few minor things we talked about earlier. Maybe 90% good/10% bad? Unfortunately that 10% is all it takes to send ripple effects of evil and darkness into the world. We never know how much impact our one small act can have, especially since we probably aren't the only dose of evil that person has experienced that day. The teenager working at the coffee shop whom you cussed out and threw a doughnut at? That morning, his dad yanked him out of bed and yelled at him for forgetting to take out the garbage. Then when he got to school, the other kids made fun of the bad haircut he had to give himself and the ragged clothes he wears because his parents make him use his income to buy all the food for the family. When you took your anger from your bad day out on him, it made him feel even more useless and depressed, and who knows where he goes from there. What if your actions are the straw that finally breaks his back, pushing him over the edge to do something worse? We have all had days that have made us feel under attack from every angle. If we can remember how it feels when someone kicks us when we are already down, perhaps we can learn empathy for others whose mistakes impact our day. Evil keeps spreading and growing because every single one of us chooses (consciously or not) to put negativity and evil out into the world, sometimes on a daily basis. I'm sure that at some point in our lives, the majority of us have played a role in making someone else's day worse, so we have to start realizing that even our smallest of negative behaviors can have much more far-reaching and intense outcomes.

I know, I know, you really are trying to be a good person. You stopped doing many of the truly awful things you once did, and you are working on the rest. Unfortunately, if you keep trying to change things on your own, you will find it pretty much impossible. The temptations we face to instigate us into behaving badly are very strong. Most of us feel overworked, underpaid, and underappreciated. We do not have the time or patience to handle any additional stress in our lives, so when the little annoying things crop up, we easily have a snippy reaction. When we have an argument with our spouse, are already late for work, and we get stuck by a train, we can lose our minds. When we rush into work late and spill our coffee, then almost immediately get confronted by some problem, it's not surprising we lash out at the first person who gives us any little reason. None of these problems are big on their own, but the little things add up until we blow our top, and out spews darkness.

Our free will, coupled with our inherent sinfulness, has made us distant from God, and leads us to listen to the temptations to do these small, evil things. So how do we overcome this tendency toward evil? We have to accept Jesus's offer to pay for our sins. We have to come to a place in our minds and hearts where we believe and know that His sacrifice saved us. We have to depend on the completeness of His salvation of us and know that it is enough to set us free. We have to trust that Jesus has done all that was necessary and know that as long as we follow Him, we are saved. We have to believe in our hearts that He is Lord and know that He chose us. And now, He wants us to choose Him back.

He wants us to give our hearts and souls to Him. He wants us to give our lives over to Him. We have to surrender to Him and allow Him to represent us to the Father. He wants us to stop trying to save ourselves, or looking for other forms of salvation. We need to stop making up in our own minds whatever we imagine or think God should be, and instead read His word and learn from Him directly. He wants us to follow His teachings, and become better people. He wants to have a relationship with us. He wants us to learn to listen to His voice and follow His light, pulling us out of our cages, and to tune out the voices of darkness trying to pull us back in. So during the sinner's prayer, we ask that His Holy Spirit will come into our hearts and change us. We tell Him that we surrender ourselves to Him and choose to live for Him now instead of living for evil. We state our belief and truth that God sent His only Son, Jesus Christ, to die for our sins and we thank Him for His sacrifice and mercy.

NOTES

5
Repentance and God's Forgiveness

"From that time, Jesus began to preach, and to say, "Repent! For the Kingdom of Heaven is at hand."
- Matthew 4:17

"As far as the east is from the west, so far has he removed our transgressions from us. Like a father has compassion on his children, so Yahweh has compassion on those who fear him. For he knows how we are made. He remembers that we are dust."
- Psalms 103:12-14

By now you should know for certain that you are a sinner, that you are deserving of punishment for your sins, and that Jesus has paid the price for your sins so that you can be set free. But what good is being set free if you still carry the weight of your sins every day?

If you set the criminal free, but still keep a record of all of his crimes, and the reminder of them affects his daily life, is he really free? In our current society, people with felonies often have a very difficult time finding employment, even after they have done their time and been released. They have received the punishment that was assigned to their crime, and have completed all of the requirements, but continue to face further persecution, because society never forgets their criminal record. Often, partially because of their inability to find work or housing, or sometimes just due to overwhelming guilt and lack of self-worth, many felons who had the goal of turning their life around instead end up in prison again.

Fortunately for you and me, God doesn't keep that permanent record of our sins. Once we accept the gift of salvation from the death and resurrection of Jesus, and we truly repent of our sins, He blots them out of our record. It will take personal work with the Holy Spirit living inside of you to fathom the depth and impact of the sacrifice of Jesus on your life. Each day, I realize and appreciate what He did more and more because each day, I learn more and more. It is similar to the process of repenting of my sins. As I initially started working through my life with His direction, I had many struggles with the repenting part of His commands, but I am learning to appreciate this process. Knowing that He forgives me and removes those sins from my record makes repenting so much easier.

I used to wonder why God even allows us to sin in the first place. As I have heard people say, God made us, He knew we would do these things, so He cannot blame us. If He didn't want us to sin, He shouldn't have given us the option. But God wants us to come to Him freely. He didn't want to make mindless robots who just did His bidding. He wanted us to have the option to choose our own destiny. He knew we would sin, but He also knew He had a plan to get us out of trouble when we did. We have been saved from certain death, and once again, we have been given a choice to make. We each have the ability to come to Him freely, and look to Him to meet all of our needs, or to deny Him, and look to ourselves and the things of this world to satisfy us. We have this ability because Jesus Christ chose to walk to death to pay the price for our sins, so that we would not have to suffer, but could instead have eternal life. Now that we have tasted what the serpent has to offer us, we have the opportunity to get a do-over and choose good instead of evil.

Assuming that we are choosing God, we need to know how we repent of our sins. There may be various things we must do to fully repent. The main thing though, is that we need to talk to God, through our prayers. To repent, in this case, means to sincerely feel remorse or regret for what we have done and to make amends whenever possible. If you cannot understand and admit your wrongdoing, then you cannot repent of it. This is why we spent time in previous chapters learning about our sinful nature, and confession, before fully talking about repentance. For our purposes, repentance encompasses three types of harm caused by our sins: harm to others, harm to ourselves, and harm to God.

Our sins hurt others because they add chaos and trouble into their lives. Just as our darkness can spread through our negative behaviors. When we do finally repent and choose to follow God, we can spread His love and hope of salvation instead. Our sins hurt ourselves because they keep us separated from God, feeling like we don't belong in His kingdom. But when we finally repent and accept His gift of salvation, we can be assured of our place. Our sins hurt God because He desires a relationship with us and wants us to know how much He loves us, but we push Him away instead of answering His call. He waits for that glorious day, when we return to Him and repent of our sins. He will come running to meet us and welcome us home.

One of the best ways to repent is to make an effort to put yourself into someone else's shoes. Most of us naturally see things from our own point of view, and need practice to learn how our actions affect others. We must apologize, but not like we did when we were kids, and our parents made us begrudgingly apologize to our siblings. We must apologize with our full heart. We also cannot make one of those back-handed apologies where we blame the other person in a roundabout way. For example, when we tease someone and then say, "I'm sorry that you got upset." Instead of acknowledging that whatever we did or said was wrong, and trying to understand why it made them upset, we shift the blame to the person we teased, and imply that they are too sensitive. Or, we offer a half-hearted apology, but in our minds we think it's silly because we do not think we have done anything wrong. We hear it all the time with public figures when they make an apology for something they did. Their apologies typically contain the line, "I apologize if I offended anyone," which lets us know that they do not believe what they said or did was wrong, just that some people might have, "taken it the wrong way". We often like to talk about our intent when we apologize, as in, "it wasn't my intention to hurt anyone", focusing on ourselves, instead of the feelings of the person we hurt. We think that if something we say or do would not be offensive to us, then others should not find it offensive either. These false apologies tend to do more harm than good, and therefore end up spreading animosity instead of love.

I think part of this stems from our own conscious or subconscious concerns about admitting we did something wrong, or accepting liability for our behavior. We are afraid of looking weak, or of giving in to the other side, or even just afraid that people won't like us if we admit to making a mistake. We do everything we can to save face and avoid accepting any blame. We say things we don't mean in the heat of the moment, but we fear apologizing when we cool down because we are embarrassed by how we acted. Or sometimes we just honestly don't think we have anything to apologize for.

One of the most difficult apologies for me to make was always after an argument. There have been several times where the other person started an argument, and I stayed calm for as long as I could, trying to de-escalate the situation, but then eventually lost my cool and started hurling insults back. Believe it or not, that behavior requires me to apologize just as if I had started the fight in the first place. There is no circumstance where it is OK for me to act that way. Whatever someone else does should not have the power to affect my behavior, and when I allow it to, I need to apologize. It is not at all easy, and it sometimes takes time to realize that I have done something I need to apologize for, because I find it much easier to blame the other person. After all, if they had just not started the fight, or if they would have accepted my repeated attempts to diffuse it, I would not have reached my breaking point and started yelling back. As a child of God, however, I am learning that only God should control my response to these situations, not the other people or circumstances involved. I cannot allow other people's behavior to make me do something evil, or turn away from what God expects of me.

Part of this process may bring you to your knees at certain points. I was so overcome by feelings of guilt and remorse when I first started allowing the Holy Spirit to take inventory of my sins. I could not believe I ever thought it was ok to act the way I acted, or to do the things I did. I could not believe how I treated people, and judged others, while I was guilty of far worse. I am learning that by acting in these ways, I am despising God. I am going against His commands and doing what He considers evil. Whether or not anyone else in the world ever knows about my thoughts or actions, God knows.

When He does call you out on something, listen to the lesson He teaches you. Put your own ego aside, humble yourself, allow your weaknesses to be brought to light, and learn from His infinite wisdom.

The ability to apologize (and mean it) is a lesson He calls on us all to learn, and it is one He has spent a lot of time with me on. I know it has taken a lot of work with the Holy Spirit for me to be able to admit to some of my sins, and to repent and make amends for things from my past. There were transgressions from times long forgotten that God brought to my mind during this process. Sometimes I still am surprised by something that pops up that I then have to deal with. Things I said or did thirty years ago can come back to haunt me as I work through my life with the help of the Holy Spirit.

Thankfully, God's forgiveness is as infinite as my sinfulness. The Bible contains several references to God's immense and unending mercy and love for His children. Conceptually, I think we can wrap our minds around the general idea. When we repent and return to Him, God basically wipes our criminal record clean and doesn't see our sins anymore when He looks at us. The difficulty lies in our ability to comprehend how vast that forgiveness is, and to trust in it when we think we have messed up and done something unforgivable. When God says we are forgiven, it means that our sins no longer exist, as we read in Isaiah 43:25, "I, even I, am he who blots out your transgressions for my own sake; and I will not remember your sins." He is ready to forgive you, now you just have to realize that truth. Pray and ask God to forgive you of your sins. Do not hide from them, but be open, repent, and allow Him to cleanse you and forgive you.

There are examples of God forgiving every one of the sins forbidden by the Ten Commandments. There is nothing you can do that God cannot forgive, except and unless you reject Him and His Holy Spirit. Matthew 12:31 quotes Jesus as saying, "Therefore I tell you, every sin and blasphemy will be forgiven men, but the blasphemy against the Spirit will not be forgiven men." If you say you do not want His help, you do not wish to repent and accept the gift of the Holy Spirit, there is nothing He can do to force you. You can choose to crawl back into your cage, lock the door from the inside, and keep His Holy Spirit out of your soul. He will be unable to pardon you from your fate of the death penalty. He will, however, continue to put you into situations that make hiding in your cage uncomfortable, and cause you to search for help. He will be knocking at your door, waiting for you, as he said in Revelations 3:20, "Behold, I stand at the door and knock. If anyone hears my voice and opens the door, then I will come in to him and will dine with him, and he with me." His desire is that you will hear Him calling for you, and that you will follow the sound of His voice. That you will allow Him to dwell inside of you through His Holy Spirit.

When you do, and when you allow the Holy Spirit to convict you and help you repent, He quickly demonstrates His forgiveness. Each time you learn to seek Him first when you fall back on your path, you learn a little more, and your trust in His promises grows a little stronger, so your steps become more confident. We can only know the extent of His strength through exposing our own weakness. As we experience how He saves us from each sin, we realize the magnitude of our despair and, by contrast, the greatness of His power. The more sins you become aware of, the more of His mercy and grace you are privileged to experience and receive.

NOTES

6
FORGIVENESS OF OURSELVES AND OTHERS

"Don't judge, so that you won't be judged. For with whatever judgment you judge, you will be judged; and with whatever measure you measure, it will be measured to you. Why do you see the speck that is in your brother's eye, but don't consider the beam that is in your own eye? Or how will you tell your brother, 'Let me remove the speck from your eye,' and behold, the beam is in your own eye? You hypocrite! First remove the beam out of your own eye, and then you can see clearly to remove the speck out of your brother's eye."

- Jesus (Matthew 7:1-5)

Judgment. I would argue it is one of the biggest problems facing many religious (and non-religious) people today, and probably since biblical times. I'm not talking about God's judgment either, although that should be our greater concern. I'm talking about people like me, who start to feel superior to others from time to time, and make judgments about their personal paths. Jesus certainly talks quite a bit about the hypocrisy of judging others. But for some reason, I still find myself doing it from time to time. When I would listen to sermons, I would often think of someone whom I wished was listening, because they were guilty of whatever the pastor was talking about that day. Worrying too much? Aunt Jean needs to hear that one. Cheating people in your business dealings? Definitely a message for the car dealer who sold me a lemon. I can't forget to mention all of the times I watched shows about people who were morbidly obese, or hoarders, or needed some sort of intervention, and thinking how much better I was than them. I would wonder how they could let themselves get that way, instead of recognizing how close I am to the edge. It made me a hypocrite because God is still working on my own food addictions, my own sins. Somehow I thought I was not as bad as them, because I always forced myself to stop overeating temporarily as soon as I was in danger of no longer being able to fit into my bigger clothes. I loved food and would go through constant cycles of eating absolutely everything I wanted as my weight slowly crept up, to eating no carb diets and exercising daily until I brought my weight back down. As the saying goes, 'there but for the grace of God go I.' I even used to judge the 'ride-or-die' behavior of born-again Christians, thinking they were all a bunch of crazy people. Until I became one of them!

This judgment of others is what the chapter quote is referencing. We have to recognize and appreciate the gravity of our own sins, and not worry about trying to judge and convict other people of theirs. The job of convicting people and cleansing them of their sins belongs to the Holy Spirit, not you or me. Our job is simply to share the good news with everyone we talk to, and to help encourage and support them on their path.

Since we are all or were sinners in some way shape or form, there is nothing that separates us in God's eyes. We are all deserving of being found guilty on judgment day. None of us is any better or worse than anyone else. Our job is to harvest everyone and then He will determine each of our fates according to His will. He does not ask any of us to help Him decide who is allowed in. We do not have the authority to pick and choose who learns about the gospel. He wants us to tell everyone about Him and His word, and then He will take care of the rest.

Seems like every so often, you hear about some type of local news story, such as a 12 year old getting arrested for writing something vaguely threatening on the school bathroom stall. Immediately people all over social media start commenting, "Teach these idiot kids a lesson!", "Where the heck are their parents?", and calling for the judge to "throw the book at her!" There are a few random folks who call for some sort of tolerance of the fact that kids do not have fully-formed brains at that age and cannot comprehend the ramifications of their actions, but there are very few. Almost no one calls for an investigation into the circumstances surrounding the incident. Why did the girl do it? Is there anything going on at school or home that might have triggered this? Were there other kids involved? I certainly understand safety first, and the threat must be evaluated. However, once that is over and it is found she made a horrible mistake and meant no harm, how about instead of treating her like a hardened criminal, we allow her the same opportunity that God has given us as grown men and women? We can provide appropriate consequences, but also forgive the offense.

Because how can we expect God to forgive us if we are going to hold a 12-year-old to a much higher standard than most adults? In fact, we must realize that we do not have better judgment than God, and if He can forgive all of us, and does forgive us, then who are we to hold a grudge? He must know something we don't, and part of walking on this path is learning to trust Him. We must ask Him for help to learn how to forgive those who have hurt us.

Some of us wear our sins openly. Our addiction to food becomes obvious when we are overweight. Drug addictions show in our faces, health, and behaviors. Anger manifests itself by yelling and screaming or fighting with people. Criminals who are found guilty always have a trial and public record of their crimes. It is easy for us to judge people when we can readily see their sins. But many of us forget that we keep our own sins under wraps. Our secret thoughts and desires. Our jealousy, our hatred, our lusts, and greed. We look down on people instead of dealing with our own indiscretions. Just as I was writing this, I was talking to my husband about the people I overheard gossiping about other people at church. We both sat there and judged them for gossiping. I mean, after all, if there's one place you shouldn't gossip, it should be the church, right? Then, the Holy Spirit stopped me and convicted me of the sins I was committing. Not only was I gossiping about the church people, and judging them for gossiping, but this took place the same day I spent most of my afternoon gossiping with co-workers about changes that were taking place at work. I immediately confessed to God and my husband, and repented and agreed with God that it was wrong. He cast a spotlight on the gossip we were doing, and that I had been doing, and He helped me think about the consequences. Isn't it absolutely absurd that I was sitting there judging the people at church for gossiping when I had been doing the same? But if we are honest, we can all find ourselves doing something like this at some point. We try to make ourselves look better by pointing out the flaws in others. Or we judge others for doing almost exactly the same thing we are doing. In fact, I have recently observed that most of the time, when someone's particular sin really bothers me, it is because I am also guilty of some version of that same sin. We can, and do, easily fall into the trap of becoming judgmental hypocrites and whenever we do, we need to ask the Holy Spirit to help us stop. After all, we do not want to risk being judged by the same measure we use to judge others. When I notice myself becoming annoyed or upset with someone and beginning to judge their behavior, I now try to stop, pray, and ask God to show me this sin in my own life. He is helping me see that my judgment of the sins of others is really His signal to me about changes that I need to make.

Remember how we talked about repentance and how important it was for you to show remorse and regret for your own sins? Since that is true, then of course, you might think you have to make it your job to point out the sins of the people who have hurt you, so that they can repent and ask you for your forgiveness, right? After all, as you are working through the process of recognizing your sins, you often run across one that doesn't seem like it quite applies to you. Interestingly enough, it does sound just like something your (insert relative/friend/co-worker here) needs to work on desperately! You think they just need to repent of this and apologize to you so you can forgive them. So you forward a sermon to them and wait expectantly for them to see the error of their ways and come asking your forgiveness. More likely than not, though, that never happens, and you become frustrated that they are not repenting to you like they should. Well, I'm very sorry to inform you that it doesn't work the same way for people who have sinned against you as it does for your own sins. While you have to repent and apologize to others for your sins, God expects you to forgive every single person who has wronged you, *even if they never apologize to you*. Even if they never admit to you that what they did was wrong. Even if they think that what they did was right. Even if they continue to do it to you to this day. Just like Jesus asked for forgiveness of the people who were torturing and killing Him. While they were putting

Him to death, He said, according to Luke 23:34, "Father, forgive them, for they don't know what they are doing." This is definitely an area most of us realize will take a tremendous amount of prayer and help to be able to do. It isn't exactly a 'day 1' thing.

None of us can do this without God's help. Forgiveness of this magnitude is impossible without His Holy Spirit. God's forgiveness is absolute, meaning, He does not just say He forgives us, but He erases all memory of the sin when He looks at us. Forgiveness of others is not complete until we can forget the offense, so you are working toward something higher than a human form of forgiveness. The goal is to allow the Holy Spirit to guide you to a more spiritual version of forgiveness, the type that allows you to forget the sin completely, and love the person underneath. Note that forgiving and loving someone does not always mean that you have to stay in contact with that person, but that you no longer hold their offenses in your heart, harboring anger, resentment, and judgment against them.

As Jesus said in John 20:23, "If you forgive anyone's sins, they have been forgiven them. If you retain anyone's sins, they have been retained." You determine how much someone's behaviors affect you. Holding onto a grudge, holding onto your anger, disappointment, or pain only ends up hurting you, and ultimately hurting your relationship with God. The people who abused you, took advantage of you, or mistreated you may never make amends. You may never see them again, or you might see them every day, but you must forgive them. If you continue to replay their behaviors over and over in your head every time you think about them, you will be continually allowing them to harm you. You have essentially sold yourself as a servant to the people who wronged you, because they are able to control you to this day, without even trying. I hear stories of people who still feel angry and resentful 20 years later when they think about a high school teacher who unfairly gave them detention. I personally have had trouble forgiving certain offenses, and when they pop into my head, I can begin to feel almost exactly the same emotions and stress as the day they happened. This is not good for me, and it does nothing to change the past. You might not even consciously realize it, but by not dealing with these situations or people it ends up affecting your day to day life. We lose sleep by worrying, or we avoid places where we might cause a scene. Only by asking God to help you forgive others, to move past the situation, and to drive out their impact from your life, will you be able to move forward. Ask the Holy Spirit to help you forgive like Jesus did, to learn how to completely and absolutely forgive and forget the offenses of those who have wronged you.

In addition, people are, after all, merely human, just like me and just like you. As repeatedly mentioned, every single one of us has made some mistakes in our lives, many of them pretty "big". However, if we believe the Bible, we believe that Jesus has already paid the debt for all of our sins, God has judged them as paid and forgiven, and wiped them off of our records. So is there someone out there who Jesus did not die for? Did He ever say, "I'm sacrificing for everyone except...", and then list certain types of people? Or did He tell even the repentant criminal being put to death next to Him that he would go with Him to His Father? As noted in the quote at the start of this chapter, Jesus tells us we are not supposed to judge the worthiness of our fellow humans to come home to the Father. Because if we do judge others as unworthy, the same measure we use will be used to judge ourselves. Meaning, if we say murderers are bad and should not be allowed in, but then we go around gossiping, hating one another, fighting, yelling, allowing people to starve, and more, we will also be judged in that category of murder. Jesus showed us that we must guard ourselves because when we fight with our brothers and sisters we are guilty and could also be judged.

If we want to cast accusations at others, we need to keep in mind that others may have their own accusations against us. Do you really want to stand before God and give Him the names of all of the people who wronged you, and ask Him to seek vengeance for you? Some of you are relishing that idea, but be careful. Because that means that all of the people you wronged in the past might give Him your name. The guy you cut off in traffic? That kid you teased back in school? The boss you stole a few office supplies from? The co-worker you alienated and gossiped about? Your ex? If you start digging a little, I'm sure you can come up with a long list of potential accusers. Vengeance might not be looking like such a great plan after all.

And where would we draw the line? If you had to stand at the gates of Heaven and determine who got in, who would you leave out? Maybe you would pick murderers, after all, killing someone is final, while other crimes can be at least somewhat undone. But then you start to think about the exceptions. Self-defense should be an obvious one, but as I learned in law school, people do not always agree on what constitutes self-defense, and I often found my sense of compassion tested by the way some of the cases were handled. For example, in one of my classes, I recall reading about a case where a woman had been severely beaten by an abusive husband, and she waited until he passed out, then killed him. Most courts do not excuse this type of murder as self-defense, maintaining that she should have left and called the police. But, as I and others argued in class, the wife was often afraid to leave, as the husband had tracked her down and punished her when she had done so in the past, and the police had been no help. In my mind at the time, she was not a danger to society, just a desperate woman trying to stop the abuse. But the point is, judgements like these are all relatively subjective. Our laws leave room for juries to debate guilt or innocence, and the mitigating factors of most crimes, and there are often many sides to every story. So God handles that problem pretty effectively - if you are guilty of breaking any of His laws, no matter to what degree or what defense you think you have, you are guilty. None of us can pretend to be innocent and none of us can pretend to be more righteous than anyone else, because we are all guilty. Our only hope is to rely on our salvation through Jesus Christ, because there is nothing we could do to save ourselves. God set it up this way intentionally so that none of us could claim superiority. As it was stated in Ephesians 2, verses 8-9, "for by grace you have been saved through faith, and that not of yourselves; it is the gift of God, not of works, that no one would boast."

It is not my job to judge and condemn the sins of others. I should not be pointing out someone's sin unless I have a relationship with them that allows for us to trust each other and grow together. It should arise out of a sincere, personal desire to help them understand what

Jesus calls sin, and I should be open about how He is helping me overcome the snare of my own sins. I must also be able to listen to their thoughts about my flaws, after all, we are all equal, and in need of cleansing. This journey works best when we feel safe being honest with others, not when we pretend to be righteous and holy. In Mark 10:18, Jesus asked the ruler who called Him Good Teacher, "Why do you call me good? No one is good, except one - God." Now, in that statement is a lot of meaning, which we will not fully explore here. The main point for our current purposes is that He made it clear to all of the Pharisees and upright people within earshot, as well as you and me all these years later, that not one of us is good, because we are not God. I am not a good person. You are not a good person. Your pastor and his wife are not good people. The pope is not a good person. This needs to be clear. If we are not good people then we cannot possibly judge others for not being good.

I hear some religious people say they have to be careful who they allow in their church. They exclude the random outsider who takes a chance by going to a Bible study, but is made to feel unwelcome because they 'have to guard against the wolf in sheep's clothing'. My understanding of this concept is that God warns us to be cautious about selecting those who are proclaiming themselves to be committed to God, for the purpose of acquiring teaching and leadership roles within your church. We want to make sure we do not have pastors and leaders teaching false doctrine and causing others to stray by the example they set. It does not apply to banning the new brother or sister in need, who wanders in, off the street, from sitting and listening to, and learning from God's word. We must all start somewhere, and God has the power and ability to turn anyone around, no matter how far back they have fallen. God does not want us to align ourselves with false teachers and unbelievers, or to endorse things that are sinful and mislead others. He warns us to guard against those who pretend to follow Him, but in reality attempt to lead us away from God, and the best way to do this is to know and stay immersed in His word by reading the Bible daily. It does not mean we exclude misguided souls who are asking questions and seeking knowledge.

If I make nothing else clear it should be that we do not get to judge, because we are in the same boat. Every single one of us has excuses for what we do. We feel pressure from all sides to make more money and go for the promotion at work, even if that means we work 70 hours a week and never see our family or have time to enjoy our money. We have all experienced some type of loss, heartbreak, abuse, or trauma, in addition to our everyday stress. We all are susceptible to the cultural influences of our time, encouraging us to crave material things, and to fit in or impress others by following whatever the newest trend is. We need to ask God to help us find it in our hearts to forgive people who are doing the best they can in these circumstances.

We also must forgive others because God has forgiven them, and if, for reasons known only to Him, He has not, then He assures us that vengeance is His. We, as humans, must only forgive others. We are not supposed to take matters into our own hands and seek revenge, we should allow Him to handle it. If we do not, we are acting as if we are somehow more knowledgeable about their sins than God, and that our judgment is superior to His.

He is the supreme authority. It would be similar to the Supreme Court of the United States declaring judgment on a case, but having a small local district court attempt to overrule it. He is our Creator and Savior and there is nothing hidden from Him. It is impossible for us to know more about how someone hurt us than He does. His judgment is perfect, and therefore, if He chooses to forgive or seek vengeance, we must accept that is the correct outcome, and not attempt to overrule His judgment.

By that same token, we must also learn to forgive ourselves. Many of us find that this is a million times more difficult than forgiving others. Remember the daughter in the story? We don't want her moping around wasting her time after her father restores her, and God doesn't want that for us either. We must apply that same spiritual level of forgiveness to our own sins. It breaks my heart to hear of people who repeatedly ask for God's forgiveness for the same sin over and over and over again. Once you have fully repented of stealing the candy bar, fighting with your parents, or having the abortion, for example, and you receive forgiveness, you can trust that

He has removed it from your record. It is gone. You do not have to recall and repent every past sin every time you pray, just ask for His help to stop sinning. It may also help you to put up safeguards to block you from some of your more addictive sins, and remember to turn to Him whenever you feel yourself starting to slip.

When we berate ourselves time and again for our sins, we are demonstrating that we do not have full confidence in His ability to forgive us. We feel like there must be something more we have to do to earn His mercy. We must remember that the same principles we used to help us forgive the sins of others, are also applicable to forgiving ourselves: a) we are only human, therefore we will make mistakes, b) it is not our job to judge or condemn anyone (including ourselves), and c) we certainly do not know more or better than God so if He has chosen to forgive us, it's time for us to do the same.

Feel free to go back and reread this chapter, but instead read from the point of view of forgiving yourself. Feelings of guilt and shame that eat away at us are easy obstacles for the enemy to put in our path to keep us from moving forward on our journey. If we feel unworthy of God's love, we will struggle to believe His sacrifice was enough to save us. This puts our faith at risk, and we are in danger of sliding back into our old habits. We must ask His help to forgive ourselves of our sins, so that we can be released from them, and move forward as a new person in His light. Repent, let them go, and trust that He has forgiven you.

Notes

7

BAPTISM: WATER AND THE HOLY SPIRIT

"But the Counselor, the Holy Spirit, whom the Father will send in my name, will teach you all things, and will remind you of all that I said to you."
- Jesus (John 14:26)

"It isn't for you to know times or seasons which the Father has set within his own authority. But you will receive power when the Holy Spirit has come upon you. You will be witnesses to me in Jerusalem, in all Judea and Samaria, and to the uttermost parts of the earth."
- Jesus (Acts 1:7-8)

Perhaps your eyes and ears have been opened and you are ready to take the next steps in pursuing a relationship with Jesus Christ. Baptism in water is an opportunity for you to commit to a relationship with God. It is a public, physical declaration of your choice to switch sides and follow Him, instead of following the ways of the world. Many of us were baptized, or christened, as infants, but there is no evidence in the Bible that any such baptism was traditionally done. I would guess at that point the commitment of baptism would really be one made by the parents, godparents, and witnesses to help the child walk a path with God, since obviously the child isn't old enough to make that commitment. This is not a bad thing, what a wonderful world it would be if every newborn child had a group of people who loved her so much they swore an oath to teach her about God! However, that alone will not save her soul. The Bible tells us that we must each make our own choice to follow God, and if we choose, to be baptized as adults. You do not have to wait until some special day when you are perfect to get baptized. In case I haven't made it clear yet, you will never be perfect, and the only way you can begin the process of being made better is by completely accepting

God. So you can go and get baptized right now, if you're ready.

This is not an occasion to be done half-heartedly. If your pursuit of God, and the information you have learned so far has led you to the point where you are ready to choose Him, then it is time to make it official, and baptism is a beautiful way to do that. It signifies the death of the old you, who followed darkness, and the rebirth of your soul into a new life in the light of Christ. It signifies to the world that you have decided to pursue God and His Heavenly Kingdom. If you are not ready to turn your life over to God, then you are not ready for baptism. Of course, it is OK and normal to still have questions and not fully understand God's word; you do not have to know everything to be baptized. But when you are baptized, you are making a commitment to follow Him and learn from Him and be guided by Him for the rest of your life. When you are ready, you do not need any fancy equipment or location. Many churches will baptize you the same day you ask; you may even find some believers who will take you to a river and baptize you there. It doesn't take long, and you don't have to prepare anything. Most likely, whoever is performing the baptism will ask you if you are committed to turning your life over to God, and whether you accept the salvation of Jesus Christ as the payment for your sins. Keep your focus on the Lord and let Him fill your heart. You will pray and then go under the water and come up as a new creation. At that point, you are born again into your new life following Jesus and you will walk down every road with Him.

He walks these roads with us, because when He died, He asked for His Spirit to be poured out on His faithful. Throughout these chapters, I have repeatedly mentioned calling on the Holy Spirit to help us and fill us. Understandably, this might sound confusing and a little weird to some. When I first started exploring my faith, I did not really understand that this was all real. I read and heard the words, I heard people singing about the Holy Spirit, but I had not grown up in a church where I knew people filled with the Spirit. When I did see rare portrayals of supposedly spirit-filled people, they often looked crazy to me, and seemed as if they were part of some sort of brainwashing cult rather than something truly from God. Then one day, after seeking and praying and yearning for God in my life, to see if it was all true, He filled me with His Spirit and my life was never the same again. I definitely did not have any dramatic, wailing outbursts like I remembered seeing in the media, just a powerful internal shift that changed the essence of who I was. Oh and lots of tears. This chapter will attempt to shed some light on what it means to be filled with the Holy Spirit and how it can happen for you. Inviting the Holy Spirit is an essential part of a sinner's prayer. Being filled with the Holy Spirit is what guides me and keeps me from straying off the path.

How do good parents raise their children? Think of your own children, if you are a parent, or think about lessons you might have been taught about behavior when you were a child. Perhaps a teacher or parent had to put you in time out when you hit your friend. Perhaps you take your teen's electronics away when they are disrespectful to you. Most of us teach our children that lying, stealing, and hurting people is wrong, so when one of them does it anyway, we typically provide some type of consequence for their behavior. We know that it would be inappropriate to allow children to just do whatever they want, snatching toys, hitting someone when they are angry, lying about their schoolwork, stealing gum from the store, eating endless amounts of sugar, or mouthing off. We put limits on their behavior to protect them, and to ensure that they will be able to get along well in life. So when a caring parent punishes a child for their bad behavior, they are doing it from a place of love, not because they enjoy hurting their children. While being put in time out or losing access to their group chat for a week might seem like the end of the world to your children, you know that it is only temporary, and that it is important for them to experience the consequences of their own bad choices.

But even more than that, you want them to learn how to behave properly. You want to help them change their behavior so that they do not hurt others. You teach them to use their words instead of fighting, and to say 'please' and 'thank-you' when they want something, instead of snatching and hitting to try to get it. You teach them to clean up after themselves, and to look both ways before crossing the street. You teach them that we have to be honest and pay for the things we want. You help them learn and grow in the hopes that they will become respectable, responsible adults.

This is basically the gift that we have been given in the Holy Spirit. Jesus asked God, the Father, to allow us who love Him to be filled with the Holy Spirit. In a sinner's prayer, we ask Him to come into our heart and change us. We invite the Holy Spirit to fill us and cleanse us. The job of the Holy Spirit living within us is to teach us, guide us, and refine us so that we can be cleansed of all sin and remain true to God's Word. The Holy Spirit can convict us of the things we do that are sinful, so that we can experience remorse for what we have done. He helps us repent and repair the damage we have done. He will help us understand what God wants us to do and to follow through with our calling. He will act like that good parent who helps pull us back onto the sunlit path when we start to follow the pretty butterfly, and wander off into the dark woods.

What I have learned is that I can generally comprehend all of the ideas in this book well enough on my own. I can know, in a theoretical way, that certain behaviors might be sinful, or that the Bible says we can die for our sins. But this does not necessarily indicate that I *know* what these biblical ideas really mean. Knowing something in my head is different from *knowing* it in my heart and soul. In order to begin to even scratch the surface of understanding the wisdom and glory of God, you must accept His gift of salvation and pray for help from His Holy Spirit. I can tell you from personal experience that being filled with His Holy Spirit is a real thing, and that you can also experience it for yourself and reap the full benefits of this amazing gift.

Without His Holy Spirit, I am incapable of completely and accurately applying biblical concepts to my own life. For example, there are days or weeks when I might do really well at changing some of my behaviors on my own. I stop gossiping at work, or stop arguments before they start with my family. I 'keep my eyes on Jesus' so I don't yell at other drivers. I start to feel smug about what a great Christian I am. Until I don't one day, and then I feel like a miserable failure. I have learned that whenever I take my eyes off of the Lord for even just a moment, I am so very weak, and no matter how hard I try, I will keep making mistakes. This is because the forces that are trying to keep me away from God are way more powerful than any human. However, if I invite His Holy Spirit to dwell within me, then I will have something living inside of me that is way more powerful than anything else in existence. He will remind me to return my focus where it belongs, and that I am a child of God who should not behave that way. Talk about protection and guidance!

The problems and situations we find ourselves faced with are designed to entice us into behaving badly. It is like we each have someone bombarding all of our weak spots constantly, with a nice little mix of whatever little things we find most annoying (stubbing a toe, losing our keys, traffic), combined with several festering problems (high credit card debt, issues at work), and a few major things that hit us deeply (accidents, divorces, deaths), thrown in from time to time. This constant attack is such a drain on our mental well-being, that we often struggle to believe there could be a God who loves us, and our focus gets pulled right back into the world. We are weakened and weary, and when we are in this dark state, it can be impossible to see the light of Jesus Christ showing us the way out.

How then, can we ever find our way out of the darkness? How do we survive these daily attacks? We must call upon someone stronger than us, something that is stronger than the dark forces, His Holy Spirit. God does not require us to choose to follow Him, and He will not intrude if we do not want Him involved. He does not force us to spend time in His presence. But He does call out to us. He has chosen us and He sent His son to pay the price to save us, so now it is up to us to choose Him. For most of us, the weight of our problems, our worries, and our sins brings us to our knees, and while looking for answers, we eventually realize that we need God's help. We reach the point where we know that He is our only hope, and we cry out to Him and invite Him in. I know, at least for me, and for the people in many of the testimonies I have heard, we had to find ourselves in what we considered a pretty low spot in our lives before we cried out to the Lord with all of our heart. The sooner you cry out, the sooner He can help you.

If you are going to have any belief in God, then you have to also believe in His Holy Spirit. The only way we can really identify, acknowledge, repent, and rectify all of our sinfulness, is by allowing His Holy Spirit to work in us. The only way we can faithfully apply God's word in our lives, be cleansed, and grow in our relationship with Him is to invite His Holy Spirit to live within us. There is a substantial gravity and depth to what happens to me when His Holy Spirit helps me to realize and internalize some new aspect of a biblical lesson. It becomes so much more than just a bunch of words on a page, He makes it come alive within me, so that what seemed impossible just a few months before becomes easy now.

I can remember the feeling I had when I was filled with the Holy Spirit for the first time. I had been praying and pleading for God to fix me, to give me patience, free me from my anger, guide me, show me. I was praying the sinner's prayer fervently. Until one day, it just happened. I don't really know how to describe it, other than I was overcome with a bright "white-lightness" that seemed to envelop me and I felt myself and my view of things change. My heart and soul felt different and amazing. My whole life shifted in that moment and I began the work God was instructing me to do. The Holy Spirit first gave me light, and gave me a sense of fulfillment, and instant peace. I was also suddenly filled with a new fire and zest for pursuing and praising God.

This does not mean that everything suddenly got easier for me. I certainly was not instantly perfect. God never promises an easy life to anyone, let alone His followers. This is one of the biggest temptations the devil tries to trick us with. I hear people make snarky, gleeful comments all the time when something bad happens to someone who believes in God: 'Guess their God couldn't save them!' or, 'Looks like their thoughts and prayers didn't work.' But if you read the Bible, bad things happen to God's people all the time. They were mocked and ridiculed, covered in boils, kidnapped and sold as slaves, and thrown into prisons. They had their children killed or kidnapped. They were beaten, tortured, and beheaded. The devil has power here on Earth, and he has the ability to try to keep us away from God. He has set up a world designed to destroy our souls. There is a battle going on for the soul of each and every person on this planet. We have to voluntarily allow God to save our souls from the devil, until then, we are inadvertently working for the enemy. Like the daughter in our story, many in this world are listening to the lies of the other man, the father they have unwittingly chosen, the devil. God is waiting for you to choose Him as your Father again. When you find yourself all alone, the only one you can turn to is God. He wants to bring us to that point where we have no other choice but to cry out to Him to help us when the devil strikes.

Once you decide to switch sides and give your life over to God, though, His Holy Spirit can dwell within you. This is how God's followers were able to withstand the attacks from the devil, and when you invite the Holy Spirit in, He can also begin to work within you. This is the most important part underlying all of the other concepts discussed in this book. If you try to do these activities on your own, you might find some temporary success, but eventually the attacks will be too much for you to handle by yourself and you may find yourself overcome. The only way through is with the help of the Holy Spirit.

At the start of this book, I mentioned that often I would have uncontrollable tears streaming down my face during worship. This, and similar expressions or outbursts, such as the giggles, can be part of the natural response of our soul when we have contact with the spiritual world. When we are pursuing God and are touched by the Holy Spirit, we encounter emotions we have never experienced before. Our souls have been trapped in the enemy's dark cages for so long now, that when we are finally exposed to the light, we might have a strong emotional response. We are simultaneously filled with immense joy at finally knowing God, but also immense sorrow at our sinfulness and the pain we have caused. When that happens, it is anyone's guess as to how you will manifest those emotions physically. For me it often means seemingly endless tears. I used to try to hide my tears, and felt embarrassed by them. Please do not be ashamed of your responses. They are completely natural, and anyone who truly seeks God will have their own experiences, so you are not alone. Embrace your new relationship with Him and everything that comes along with it. Delve more deeply into those emotions and ask Him to help you understand why you are reacting in these ways.

Another thing that happened to me, and to other people I have talked to, is that we were suddenly overcome by an urgent desire to 'do things' for God. I had the strong urge to read the Bible and learn as much as possible about God. I had an intense need to look for ways to help others. I wanted to tell everyone about how I had the Holy Spirit, but I also wanted to keep it to myself. I honestly felt a little overstimulated for a while. Like I was buzzing with an energy at a level I had never experienced before in my life. I felt pulled in so many directions, probably because there was so much work to do to heal my soul. Even though this sounds and felt very overwhelming, I also felt a peace about it all. I felt joy and happiness even though everything in my life was far from idyllic. I felt renewed, but also charged and expectant that something big was happening to me. I have difficulty describing the feelings I had during this time because I have never experienced anything like it. I had all of the Spirit, but I was still learning how to focus my attention, and do what I was supposed to with all of His energy and power flowing through me. Being filled with the Holy Spirit can provide us with many benefits, but, as usual, it will take time and commitment to really understand the power we have been given and to experience the full magnitude of these gifts.

I know this may sound very strange and supernatural. It is. It is like nothing you or I have ever known before, and when one day, you realize the truth of it all, it will do some crazy things to you. God starts us on an incredible journey when we invite Him into our hearts. I am still making mistakes and learning every moment, but I also continue to grow every day as I walk with God.

It is a real thing. You will know when it happens. Pursue Him and call out to Him and He will answer. The time is short, so do not wait. We never know the day when we will die, or when Jesus will come back, so we must be prepared at all times. Pray for, and seek the Holy Spirit. Ask Him to enter into your heart and help you as you pursue a relationship with Him. He will only come to those who invite Him. Those who choose Him.

NOTES

8
GRATITUDE

"Oh give thanks to Yahweh, for he is good, for his loving kindness endures forever."
- 1 Chronicles 16:34

"Oh come, let's sing to Yahweh. Let's shout aloud to the rock of our salvation! Let's come before his presence with thanksgiving. Let's extol him with songs! For Yahweh is a great God, a great King above all gods. In his hand are the deep places of the earth. The heights of the mountains are also his. The sea is his, and he made it. His hands formed the dry land."
- Psalms 95:1-5

Finally, no sinner's prayer would be complete without an expression of gratitude to God. One of the things we often say when we pray is, 'thank you'. I know, from first-hand experience, unfortunately, that thanking God might be difficult for some of us, especially if we have suffered a tragedy, abuse, or illness in our lives. We may find it hard to find a reason to be thankful to God and we struggle to see any blessings in our life. Sometimes we even find ourselves cursing or questioning Him when something bad happens to us or someone we love. Showing gratitude to God doesn't always come naturally. After all, if we learn that God is in full control, and everything that happens to us is part of the perfect will of God in our lives, then it is certainly understandable why we might feel less than grateful when we are faced with trying times.

As I mentioned previously, though, life is always going to present us with challenges. There are different reasons for these challenges, depending on where we are in our walk with God. Often, before we have made the commitment to Him, we are presented with trials that are designed to bring us to Him. Other times, we might be learning how to navigate obstacles to our faith. Still other times, God might be allowing the devil to tempt you to try to pull you away from His love and back into your cage on the other side. No matter what, we can trust God that there is always a purpose to our suffering and trials, and that purpose is always designed by God to work out for our ultimate good.

One reason I have learned to be thankful to God, even during times of trial and tribulation, is that I have seen first-hand how many of those things I thought were roadblocks, eventually turned out to guide me to a better destination. I have seen evidence that what God has planned is always better than my original plans. Take, for example, the time I prayed for, but did not get, a job that would have meant a $20,000 a year raise and a shorter commute. This was something that I was certain would have been a considerable blessing to my family. I was devastated and brewed over my mistakes in the interview for quite some time. I would sometimes imagine what I could be doing with the extra money and feel resentful. Of course, as I later learned, God knew that was not the best path for me.

Not getting the job turned out to be a blessing in disguise. Less than two years later, that position was eliminated. Not to mention, I spoke with a friend who had been working in the same department, but left because they were not treating her well. When I first learned that I did not get the job, my reaction should have been one of thanking God for seeing what I could not see, and knowing what I did not know, rather than feeling upset. I should have been rejoicing because of my trust in God, instead of wallowing about the money I could have made. I have learned to accept and be grateful for things like the death of loved ones, because it means that it was part of God's plan to call them, and their suffering is over. I have learned to try to be grateful for pain that has come into my life, because I know that God is teaching me something through my pain. Many of you are probably not at this point yet, and that is OK. I was not at first either, and to be honest, I still have plenty of moments where I find myself complaining, or getting angry and annoyed. But even if we aren't quite at the point where we can sing "hallelujah!" through every single turmoil, there are still ways we can see and be thankful for the good things God has provided in our lives.

When I listen to society in general, it seems like we constantly complain about all of the things we don't have. We love to pray for lottery winnings and financial blessings, as if that will be what saves us. But if you think about it, would you really enjoy sitting around doing nothing for the rest of your life while other people serve you, pay for all of your desires, and do everything for you? I know the old me would have said, "Absolutely! Sign me up!", but I would have been wrong. As I have grown, I have learned some things about the hidden dangers of such a lifestyle.

First of all, having expensive things is not all it's cracked up to be. I used to spend way more money than I needed to, on things I tried to convince myself were necessities. This tendency of living beyond my means left me constantly broke. I do not need that many shoes, that much square footage, or a brand new car. We can eat the majority of our meals at home and actually eat our leftovers. I do not need to have a mani/pedi ever. I once heard about someone who made millions, bought a mansion, and absolutely hated it. There was always something breaking down, and so much work to do to maintain the house, that he constantly had employees in his home. He could never just relax because there were people there, all the time, and of course, this was all very expensive. And don't underestimate the problem of getting lost in your own home, or how far the walk to your master bathroom would be at 4 am. That one of a kind luxury sports car? It's practically ruined by one scratch, and an oil change can cost more than my current car is worth. There are plenty of things we can desire, or waste our money and energy on, but in the end, they often come with more problems than they solve. And, when we pass on, all of those material possessions will eventually crumble and decay. You cannot take them with you, and they cannot fulfill you, because they do not have any intrinsic value.

Secondly, having no purpose in life to wake you up each day seems like it only leads to trouble. Living life on a permanent vacation is not a blessing, it's a curse. So many of the rich and famous seem to wind up with drug and alcohol dependency, depression, wild lifestyles, or early death. Yes, travel, taking classes, and enjoying a pampered life would seem fun for a while, but eventually, even that gets old. Your current friends would not be able to keep up with your new lifestyle, and so you would end up spending time with others who could afford the time and money to do the same things you can. You might pay their way for your less financially blessed friends who join you, but you would soon start to wonder who was just there for the benefits. You would look for more and more unique and extreme ways to spend your time and money, because the thrills are no longer as exciting as they once were. Without a purpose for your life and work to do each day, you grow restless.

Furthermore, once you start chasing money and possessions, there never seems to be enough to satisfy. We ask this about the very wealthy all the time, "How much is enough? How rich do they have to be?" We see CEO's of mega-corporations and celebrities make billions by overcharging the rest of us for their products and services. They seem to have everything, and then some, but they still want more. They accumulate fleets of outrageously expensive cars, huge homes in several countries, private jets, and still want to raise the prices we pay. We can easily see how greed controls them, but the question then becomes, how do greed and envy control you? How much is enough for you? When will you be satisfied with what you have and stop being envious of those who have more? The truth is, no matter how much we accumulate, it will never be enough to fulfill us because what we are missing is not material wealth, it is spiritual wealth, in the form of God's love.

Stop longing for that life, it will never fulfill you, and to be honest, when you long for a pampered life, you sound like a child, wanting other people to do everything for you. Vacations are fun for a reason, because they are temporary. They give us a little break from having to take care of ourselves for a while. They allow us time to take a mental pause so we can come back to reality with a fresh outlook. But living that life every day is not going to give you the joy and satisfaction you think it will. And dwelling on money and material possessions is keeping you from being grateful to God, because it is blinding you to the blessings He has given you. It is making you resentful for material wealth. If you are looking for earthly, material rewards from God, you should realize that He would much prefer to give you eternal rewards. Free your mind from the trap of not feeling blessed because you don't have a walk-in closet full of designer clothes, a fleet of vehicles, and a model-spouse.

As you look around and see all of the beauty in nature, a sunrise, a flower garden, snow on the trees, you realize what a magnificent creation God has made for us. When you think of all of the varieties of food He has given us, that simply grow out of the ground, you realize how well He has provided for us. If you really consider what we have, you will realize that we are wealthier, and have more assistive technology at our hands than most rulers at any time throughout history. For example, we have year-round refrigeration, and ice cream on demand! That would have been a miracle back in the days when they had to retrieve ice from mountains. In the United States, we generally have clean running water, we can travel to other places relatively easily, and we have access to more varieties of food and spices than at any time before. The small things we take for granted as ordinary, are actually miraculous when you stop and really think about them.

Sunlight alone is enough to thank God for, so we can definitely sing His praises for all of these wonderful things.

Of course, as we have discussed, the main reason we can praise God is to thank Him for the gift He has given us in Jesus Christ. He sent His Son to die for us as payment for our sins. He endured mental and physical torture and pain. He died slowly and willingly to save us. If someone saves your life, the very least you can do is thank them and praise them for what they have done. He is worthy of your praise for that reason alone, as it is only by His sacrifice that we are even able to make the choice to follow Him. We need His blood to wash away our sins.

We are supposed to praise and worship God. We are supposed to give Him all of the honor and glory for everything that happens in our lives. Unfortunately, many of us spend all day wishing we had someone else's clothes, body, hair, car, relationship, or house instead of focusing on what really matters. We ignore our blessings because we think someone else got more. The more you pursue God and follow His light to walk on the path, the more you will find to be grateful for, and you will one day find it difficult to contain your praises. If it is still a struggle for you right now, start with the basics. If you ate food today, even if it was just the stale granola bar from the bottom of your purse, thank Him for that food. If you had a place to sleep last night, thank Him. If you had clothes and shoes to wear today, or warm water for a shower, give Him praise. If you had to go to work today, thank Him that you have the mental and physical ability to make money to provide for your needs. Even if the rest of the day is rough, or things aren't going as planned, give Him your honor. We should be rejoicing in what we do have, not worried every day about what we do not. Envy is a rabbit hole of distraction that leads us away from God. Rejoice in his blessings and praise Him instead!

NOTES

9
THE END

"Yahweh looked down from heaven on the children of men, to see if there were any who understood, who sought after God."
- Psalms 14:2

"One thing I have asked of Yahweh, that I will seek after: that I may dwell in Yahweh's house all the days of my life, to see Yahweh's beauty, and to inquire in his temple."
- Psalms 27:4

Phew. That was a lot. At least, it felt that way to me, as I tried to put these concepts into words. Explaining the very personal and unusual experiences that happen as we begin our journey from belief in God, to the pursuit of life in His Kingdom, is not straightforward. All I can do is pray that I have done it some justice on these pages, and that God will use this book in His way to bring people to Him. I pray that it helps you on your faith journey, and that, like the daughter in our story, you will allow your Father to help you find your way home.

When God came into my life, everything changed. I began working with Him through the process of cleansing my soul and becoming more like Jesus. I know now 100% that my life was saved by the sacrifice of Jesus Christ, and that I have a place with Him in the Father's House. I desperately want this for you too. I pray that He will do for you what He is doing for me. I pray that you want that for yourself and are willing to seek Him. We are all sinners, who are unable to save ourselves. No amount of good works could ever make up for the bad we have done. But God loves us so much, He is willing to forgive us, and so He saved us by using the blood of Jesus Christ to pay the ransom to free our souls. Now the choice is up to each one of us what we do with our freedom. Do we choose darkness and remain in our cages, or choose to run out into His light and follow Him?

Pursue God by subjecting yourself to starting the journey outlined in these chapters. Read the Bible every day. Take a break from secular TV and radio and instead listen to lessons on His word, and to music praising the Lord (it's actually really good!). Pray about every need or concern you have. When you find yourself questioning, doubting, confused, hurting, or lost, call out to Him and listen for His answer. Apply the lessons you learn to your daily life, and allow God to start to change you. He knows what He must do to equip you for what is coming up next on the path. He can see what is around the bend, where we cannot. As we journey to pursue God's kingdom, we have to remember that. We have to trust that by working through the steps outlined in this book, He is preparing us for what lies just outside of our view. We become what we pursue. If we pursue the path of chasing worldly pleasures like material wealth, power, and our sexual desires, we will become consumed by them. If we chase after the path of the Lord, we will become consumed by Him. This is the fork in the road, and it is impossible to walk both directions at the same time. Which path will you pursue?

Dear Heavenly Father,

Please help all of us choose to pursue Your path. Please guide and protect all of us as we journey on our path to Your home. Please open the hearts, eyes, and minds of everyone who reads this book, so we can know Your glory and pursue a relationship with You. Please help us to recognize and repent of our sins, and to understand our salvation through Jesus Christ. Please help us to stay strong in our faith as we pursue Your teaching. Please help us to learn and grow as we read Your word. We thank You for all of the blessings You have given us and we praise You now and forever.

Amen.

NOTES

About the Author

 Elizabeth was a sinner, turned child of God, who is on a mission to share the good news of our salvation through Jesus Christ. She writes books in obedience to God's will, praying that they will help others seek God. She lives a simple life in Michigan with her family, and has had careers as both a lawyer and teacher. She believes all honor and glory are reserved for the Lord, and seeks to love God and love people in accordance with His commandments. She welcomes you to email savedsisterinchrist@gmail.com if you have any questions about your personal journey.

Books in the Logic to Rest series:
Logic to Belief
Belief to Pursuit
Pursuit to Commitment (coming 2024)